BEING TOGETHER
The Rebirth of the Piazza

by

Barry B. Scherr

SUNDAR

SUNDAR

Being Together - The Rebirth of the Piazza by Barry B. Scherr

Published by Sundar Publishing - A Subsidiary of Sundar Corporation

Arcetri, LLC   http://www.arcetripiazza.com

First Edition: May 25, 2022

ISBN: 978-1-7923-9230-6

For details or further information, please contact us at: barry@arcetripiazza.com

BEING TOGETHER

THE REBIRTH OF THE PIAZZA FOR THE 21ST CENTURY

TABLE OF CONTENTS

PART ONE - THE BIRTH OF THE PIAZZA

PART TWO - THE REBIRTH OF THE PIAZZA

BEING TOGETHER

As the pace of paradigm-changing technological progress accelerates, we need a counterbalancing real estate structure that brings people together. Our solution is the Arcetri Piazza, a blueprint for a new asset class structured around our intrinsic need to be together. The design is based on the historic piazzas of the Italian peninsula updated to become the central meeting place for the 21st century.

INTRODUCTION

This book is the culmination of 35 years of life experience and research into what brings people together and makes communities livable. What is an ideal built environment? What is ideal living? What makes us happy, healthy, and helps us on our journey towards enlightenment? To find answers to those questions, I travelled to 28 countries and criss-crossed most of the United States.

Today the commercial real estate world is experiencing an existential crisis. Old ways of thinking and doing are being swept away. People, both young and old, want more human-centric built environments that match their evolving lifestyles.

My personal study of these issues began with my last paper in college which explored ideas about the growth of consciousness and world lifestyle trends. After college, I entered the commercial real estate business. In 1988, I was invited to a series of meetings for real estate professionals where Maharishi Mahesh Yogi — the renowned Indian teacher who popularized Transcendental Meditation™ — presented his ideas on the built environment. He had come to the conclusion that there had been inadequate planning in existing cities and towns worldwide. I remember how startled I felt when Maharishi suggested that the built environment needed to be completely rebuilt. Now, thirty years later, we find ourselves at a junction point, where there will be a massive reconfiguration of the built environment due to property and infrastructure obsolescence.

My real estate career launched as the big-box retail revolution was just beginning. As the various category-killers emerged, local retail suffered as the public was mesmerized by the size and wide selection, and convenience of the grab 'n go system.

BEING TOGETHER

THE REBIRTH OF THE PIAZZA

Over time, I realized the limitations of this unidimensional approach to not just retail, but of the whole commercial real estate world. Along the way, I've had many encounters and experiences that have given me pieces of the puzzle that make up the ideas in this book. I have spent much of my life living in three different cultures: the economic and creative powerhouse of Southern California, the ancient, warm and beauty-based Italy, and the relaxed, sun-drenched landscape of Florida. The contrasts I have experienced between these diverse cultures have helped open my mind and heart, and contributed to this vision for the ideal asset class: the Arcetri Piazza.

I spent years walking and exploring Rome, Florence, Venice, Lucca, Paris, London, New York and Los Angeles. During that time, I slowly began to gain a new understanding of what the elements of an ideal lifestyle could be. A picture emerged of a world that requires a different point of view with revised priorities. The realization of this new paradigm will require the collective vision of mayors, planners, developers, bankers, architects, educators, business people, and concerned citizens.

The Arcetri Italian Lifestyle Piazza as presented in this book is the culmination of these many years of collecting pieces of the puzzle. The complete picture of what it takes to recreate the wonderful feeling I experienced in streets and piazzas became clear: a feeling a part of something bigger, and more beautiful.

This book introduces a new asset class that resolves the conflict between cash flow and providing an environment that people really want, an asset class for the newly evolving 21st Century lifestyles.

Barry B. Scherr
West Palm Beach, Florida - Florence, Italy – 2021

PART ONE

THE BIRTH OF THE PIAZZA

Forget Everything You Knew About the Piazza!

4

BEING TOGETHER

THE REBIRTH OF THE PIAZZA

Forget Everything You Knew About the Piazza!

A piazza is much more than a place to have a coffee, lunch or go shopping. It's the multi-faceted central reference point for a neighborhood, community, or city. Today it is more important than ever to reintroduce this tried and true concept. While modern technology connects us to the world through the internet and high-speed travel, thus eliminating the limitations of time and space, we are experiencing an urgent need to once again learn how to be together, share together and see and listen to each other.

Human life, culture and habitat are designed for our safety, security, connection and evolution. Today the culture of family life that has bound us together forever has been loosened in favor of individuality, flexibility and opportunity. This trend is creating a worldwide crisis of disconnection that needs to be balanced by a new type of place that creates a new reason for being together.

The Arcetri Italian Lifestyle Piazza provides the structure to offset and stabilize the 24/7 lifestyle that has become the standard for modern living.

Now let's consider both the structure and the culture of a new vision of the piazza built on the past, but with a new intention for wellness, connection and a daily routine that make sense.

The Story of Life Is the Story of Giving and Sharing.

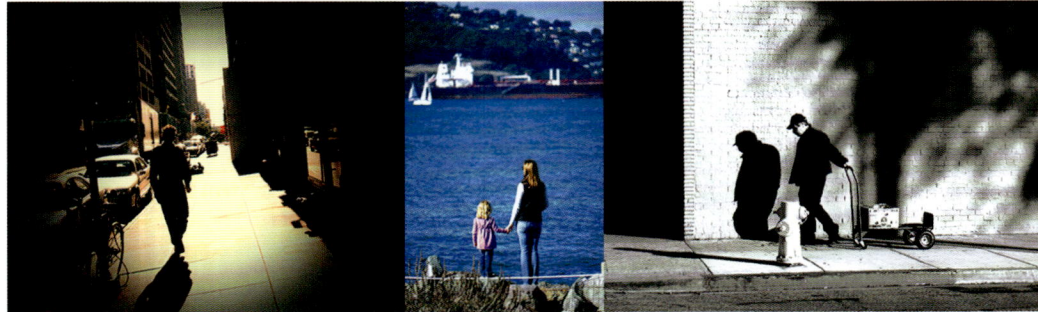

As society has grown more and more anonymous, the drive for individual recognition has accelerated. Everyone craves to be appreciated, heard, understood and loved. Life flows in the feelings we have for each other, ourselves and society. Being together means we are part of a wholeness of life, a field of love. This includes friendship, acceptance and mutual recognition of each other. It means that, in our busy lives, we have enough time to spend a moment in each interaction greeting the beauty, intelligence and potential of each other.

Some years ago, an Englishman - disenchanted with civilization - decided to live by himself on a deserted island. After some time, he finally returned to the civilized world. He was asked by a reporter why, and he responded that it was too painful not having someone with whom to share the immense beauty of the island.

We love to share. It increases our joy and makes bearable our sorrows and loss. And, the other side of giving is that we encounter an endless stream of energy and goodwill. Being together in this context means evolving together, seeing the beauty in each other, confirming each other's value and legitimizing our status as children of God.

Never lonely, never without love - this is being together.

BEING TOGETHER

THE REBIRTH OF THE PIAZZA

Truly being together means that we are never lonely, we enjoy a meal with friends and family, we go to the piazza to see and be seen. In this way, we become part of something bigger than ourselves: inspired by the beauty, admiring the power of the architecture, immersed in the present, not rushing off, surrounded by the energy of other humans engaged in the beautiful drama of life.

This is our natural ecosystem: where we can enjoy being together while pursuing our individual needs without friction, without traffic, without obstacles. The underlying precondition for being together is this: as people become more rested, sensitive, and happier, they find greater joy in socializing and developing meaningful friendships. It is a self-reinforcing cycle of goodness and benefit.

The Arcetri Piazza welcomes people: it makes space for them to come in and participate. It's where we come to experience the layers of meaning within every interaction, while our feelings become enlivened as we enjoy the process of our consciousness and happiness growing.

A BRIEF HISTORY OF THE PIAZZA

If piazzas are so great, how come no one builds them anymore?

Since Roman times, the piazza design became widespread and was originally shaped by the Roman's habit of creating marketplaces wherever their imperial roads intersected. Over time, these markets coalesced into central civic spaces. It is this basic design that has existed for thousands of years in one form or another.

The structure of togetherness and sharing has always had a design based on the human scale.

The use of piazzas reached its apex in the Italian Renaissance as the center of city states, and over the ensuing centuries gradually devolved into main streets and plazas. The classical Piazza originated in a time when daily life was much simpler, when walking was the norm rather than the exception. By the mid-20th Century, the automobile allowed us to go every which way without regard to the center. The piazza as the central organizing place - the heart of every neighborhood - was mostly lost.

BEING TOGETHER

THE REBIRTH OF THE PIAZZA

MISURA HUMANE - THE HUMAN SCALE

The Age of the Automobile is coming to an end and a New Age of Walking is being rediscovered.

In piazza-centered developments people mostly walk to accomplish their daily needs and see friends and family along the way.

The Misura Humane is an ancient architectural scale that was born in an age when people lived and walked in the course of their everyday life.

The Arcetri Piazza development concept will allow for the embrace of the Walking Life - an enlightened lifestyle answer to today's energy and climate crisis.

MISURA HUMANE - THE HUMAN SCALE
A PERSONAL PERSPECTIVE

One day, I was walking through Rome and, after I descended the Spanish Steps and made my way to Via Condotti, one of Rome's most fashionable streets, I was window shopping and very much enjoying the relaxed Roman atmosphere.

After a while, I entered a shop where I encountered a young clerk. I remarked to her how much I was enjoying the wonderful feeling that seemed to emanate from the compact proportions of the street and surrounding shops. Without missing a beat, she replied, "Ah signore, but this is the misura humane – the human scale. It is because these streets were built before cars. They were built for human beings." This casual statement – something that seemed perfectly obvious to her - struck me with the full force of a fundamental revelation. It changed the course of my thinking forever.

THE PASSEGGIATA

pas.seg.gia.ta

/.pas'jada/

Italian noun

1.   a leisurely walk or stroll, especially one taken in the evening; a promenade (used with reference to the tradition of taking such a walk in Italy or Italian-speaking communities, and other Mediterranean cultures.)

When one immerses oneself in a Mediterranean culture – especially Italian – one of the most charming and powerful experiences is to participate in a passeggiata - an evening ritual which takes place in the narrow connecting streets between piazzas. It's a way of connecting with neighbors and the greater community. These days, it's an antidote for the enhanced disassociation brought on by the automobile culture. When neighbors walk through these narrow streets each evening, they encounter one another in a relaxed social space. This creates a common experience, a sense of connection, as well as maintaining a healthful evening exercise tradition.

THE PASSEGGIATA

This ancient, distinctly human activity has been practiced by communities around the world, where people tend to want to walk outside in a social setting after the evening meal. It is an intergenerational activity, with older people and married couples circulating and socializing, often with their dogs along for the ride. At the same time, there will be a separate strata of young adults also walking in the evening, alongside but slightly separate from the older people, preoccupied with flirting, sizing up potential mates, and seeing friends. And then a third strata swirls amongst them, made up of children circulating freely within this larger, older crowd – playing, making mischief and generally just being kids.

THE PIAZZA IS CENTRAL TO HUMAN CIVILIZATION

Today we are in the process of a Second Renaissance where technology fulfills its potential to take away the repetitive tasks and other routine work of everyday life, leaving us time to grow, create and enjoy our lives. The Arcetri Piazza is the perfect technology to help make this possibility a reality.

Illustration of the Arcetri Garden & Event Piazza

13

THE PIAZZA IS CENTRAL TO HUMAN CIVILIZATION

Thousands of years ago, as the practice of agriculture took hold, people began to live in villages that, over time, grew into towns and cities. This increase in population density ultimately gave people more time to develop highly specialized skills.

This culture, generated over millennia of working together, eating together, and simply being together, is deeply embedded within our DNA. For thousands of years, it had been a matter of survival, and as time went by, these fundamental family and clan relationships nurtured and cultured our intelligence.

Over these millennia, with the notions of accumulations of wealth, land ownership and international trade, writing became a necessity. We evolved highly developed language skills, a new sense of time, new dietary habits, hierarchical social structures, and the concept of private property.

This resulted in a massive wave of transformation. Friendship, family life, and business life developed a diverse set of emotions and knowledge necessary to navigate daily life successfully in this more urban, human-centric world.

The culture of Being Together is deeply embedded within our DNA.

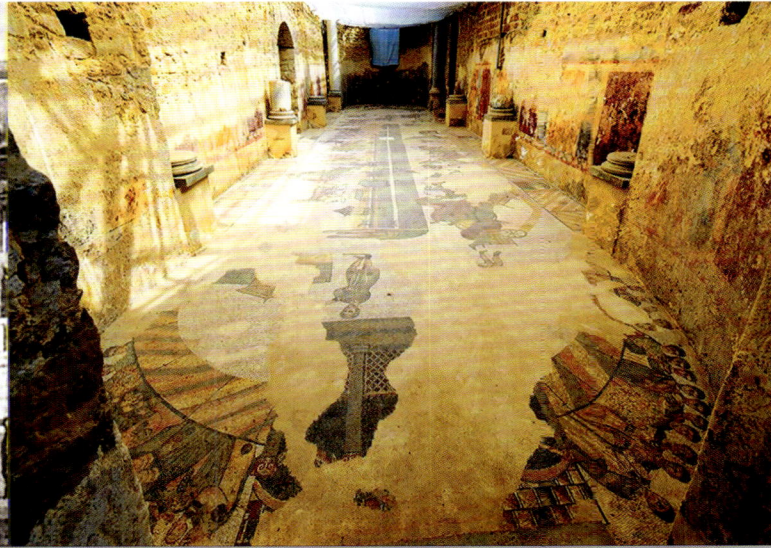
THE PIAZZA IS CENTRAL TO HUMAN CIVILIZATION

As we became less intimately intertwined with nature, we gradually asserted our own individuality as separate from nature. We began to put our trust more and more in our understanding of the laws of nature and our ability to develop technologies to control the environment.

Ancient Greek Agora

Early Italian Piazza

A descendant of the classical Greek agora, the Italian piazza became a technology for people to maintain the integrity of their community as part of their daily lives within the wider context of increasing specialization, more efficient agricultural practices and the explosion of international trade. In fact, the remarkable rise of a newly prosperous merchant class that occurred in places like Florence, Venice and Pisa during this period was a key element in supporting the success of the piazza.

15

THE PIAZZA IS CENTRAL TO HUMAN CIVILIZATION

"FUTURIST" ITALIAN ART OF THE EARLY 20th CENTURY

"il Trittico della Velocita" 1927 - Gerard Dottori   "Dynamism of a Car" 1913 Luigi Russolo

The natural empathy and compassion we felt for one another for tens of thousands of years began to gradually erode as our communal/nature-centric sense of self began to transform into a more individualistic/urban orientation. With the relatively recent advent of the 19th Century Industrial Revolution and then the 20th Century Technology Revolution, we have seen a profound acceleration of that sensibility to the point where personal isolation and loneliness have become a major problem around the world.

THE PIAZZA IS CENTRAL TO HUMAN CIVILIZATION

During the Renaissance, the piazza became a much-loved city center around which people were able to develop a graceful style of living that helped balance the relentless shift towards a more worldly, commerce-based society that emphasized individual intiative.

"The Flower Market in Piazza delle Erbe, Verona Italy" by Albert Goodwin (circa 1920)

The piazza became the heart of the city and public life. Personal feelings, relationships and interaction were naturally renewed in the piazza, and enlivened on a daily basis. Originally built in an age of walking and horses, the overall space of a piazza, and its surrounding streets, have a distinctly human sense of proportion and comfort. These urban spaces were built to serve every human need including social interaction, daily markets, religion and even politics.

17

THE PIAZZA IS CENTRAL TO HUMAN CIVILIZATION

Now, in our present-day automobile-centric, consumer culture, we have lost these essentially human experiences, much to the detriment of our physical and emotional well-being.

We are developing the Arcetri Piazza as a time-tested structure where one can be together in a field of love, friendship and purpose while simultaneously pursuing one's daily needs and ambitions, hopes and dreams.

Illustration of an Arcetri Lifestyle Piazza

When you build for the long-term, architecture can give people
a sense of timelessness and unexplored possibilites.

THE PIAZZA IS CENTRAL TO HUMAN CIVILIZATION

When you visit the piazza as a tourist or in the course of your daily routine, there is an overwhelming sense of being part of something grand, beautiful and bigger than oneself while enjoying the rhythms and patterns of daily life.

In the piazza, one is simultaneously part of the whole and also contributing to the various parts, just as people have done for centuries. Even the physical proportions of the piazza - generally rectangular or square - create a space that generates coherence and flow for maximum multi-dimensional interactivity. The central part of the piazza supports a variety of activities over time, while the perimeter marks the boundary area within which restaurants and businesses can be situated - easy to access and enjoy.

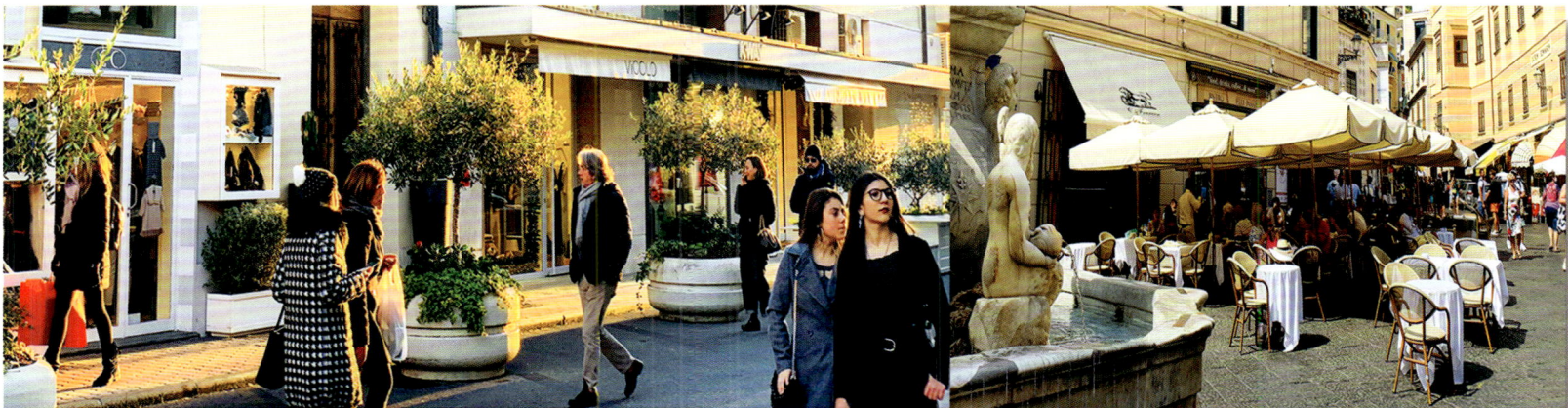

*The piazza provides easy access to all the daily necessities
in a dedicated space that celebrates life.*

The rise of individuality has meant that we have lost something essential - the experience of belonging to something greater than oneself.

Not so long ago the exaltation of individuality was rare, and the identity of the group predominated...

BEING TOGETHER
THE REBIRTH OF THE PIAZZA

THE RISE OF THE INDIVIDUAL

How the Rise of Individuality, along with City States of the Italian Peninsula during the Renaissance, led to the Lessening of Community Life by the 21st Century

> "To the discovery of the outer world, the Renaissance added a still greater achievement, by first discerning and bringing to light the full, whole nature of man"
>
> "Civilization of the Renaissance in Italy" - Jacob Burkhardt

Over the vast millennia of human life on earth, people have mostly lived in small communal groups – family or clan – and the notion of the individual as an ascendant identity is a very recent phenomenon.

The idea of the individual as a separate entity with its own significance, and even destiny, only came to the fore during the Renaissance. This was accompanied simultaneously by the recognition of individual genius (Leonardo da Vinci, Galileo, Michelangelo, etc.). Prior to that, great artists were very rarely credited or publicly recognized. They almost never signed their works.

21

THE RISE OF THE INDIVIDUAL
THE DISCOVERY OF PERSPECTIVE

Within the worlds of Renaissance science and art, the revolutionary discovery and utilization of the laws of perspective served to heighten this awareness and, along with that came the understanding of the primacy of the individual and the individual perspective. For, without recognizing the importance of the individual, there would be no single point-of-view, which is the basis for understanding perspective. The Vanishing Point is always in reference to a single observer's point-of-view. And, indeed, when the observer moves, the Vanishing Point's position moves in lockstep with the observer.

In today's world, this seems obvious almost to the point of cliché, but, in fact, this was a revolutionary discovery. Aside from changing the style and even conceptual framework of murals and paintings, it discreetly established the prominence of the individual. Suddenly there was such a thing as a "point of view".

THE RISE OF THE INDIVIDUAL

Looking at the many thousands of years of artistic accomplishment from around the world prior to this discovery, it is striking to note the near-total lack of perspective in every form of visual expression. For all those thousands of years, practically every visual representation is presented in a flat, planar space, often to great aesthetic effect, but still within a conceptual framework that lacked the individual perspective. This clearly transmitted the basic fact that people were rarely, if ever, seen as distinct from their family, clan or village.

Individuals were experienced as being part of the pattern of life.

BEING TOGETHER

LIVEABILITY

SUSTAINABLE

WELLNESS
SERVICES

COMMUNITY

WALKABLE

MARKET
DAILY SHOPPING

GATHERING
& EATING

SOCIAL
POLITICAL

TRADE

TRANSACTIONAL

| VILLAGE CROSSROADS 3000-1000 BC | AGORA 600 BC - 400 AD | RENAISSANCE PIAZZA 1400 AD - PRESENT | INTERNATIONAL CITY CENTERS 15TH - 20TH CENTURY | TOWN SQUARE 18TH - 20TH CENTURY | U.S. URBAN DOWNTOWNS 19TH - 20TH CENTURY |

TIME

24

REBIRTH OF THE PIAZZA

HOPPING
MALLS
1956

BIG BOX RETAIL
1986 - LATE
20TH CENTURY

ENTERTAINMENT
CENTERS
IRVINE SPECTRUM,
THE GROVE
1995- PRESENT

IMMERSIVE RETAIL
1995 - PRESENT

RESTAURANTS/
COFFEE SHOPS
PLAZAS
19TH CENTURY -
PRESENT

ARCETRI PIAZZA
21ST CENTURY

THE BIRTH OF THE PIAZZA
THE AGORA

The rise of the institution of the agora in classical Greece marked the birth of the piazza in Western civilization. The agora was a centrally located area within a city, where all sorts of people met and conversed, argued, and philosophized. Originally – and for thousands of years – the forerunner of the agora was almost certainly the local place to access well water along with the communal fire. In communities around the world, this was where gossip, stories and news were exchanged and friendship bonds developed. Eventually communities grew up around such essential meeting-places and these, over time, developed into important social centers.

THE BIRTH OF THE PIAZZA
THE AGORA

As villages became larger, marketplaces naturally sprung up around these areas and the centrality of the water-well and market became ever-more firmly established as the cultural/social center for communities around the world. With the rise of larger towns and then cities, these central areas become more formalized and by 600 B.C. in Greece, the agora was born. It was in the agora that Socrates, Plato, Aristotle, Pythagorus, Aeschylus and many others interacted and eventually developed the foundational Western notions of science, arts and democracy.

The Romans held Greek culture in high regard and, in the course of creating their cities, they clearly used the notion of the agora to establish their own grand Imperial plazas. The Roman Forum was conceived as a super-agora, where all the important civic meeting places were convened to most efficiently facilitate the running of the vast Roman Empire.

THE BIRTH OF THE PIAZZA

THE AGORA

One of the foundational notions of the Renaissance was the rediscovery of many aspects of classical Greek culture. This included a revival of the philosophies of Plato and Aristotle, as well as many of the scientific and cultural accomplishments from Classical Greece.

The infusion of the profoundly potent ideas from Classical Greece, combined with the recognition of the individual, and the resulting celebration of individual "genius", helped bring the Renaissance into full flower.

It is this synergistic combining of the many cultural and scientific developments of the Renaissance that over time produced the many and varied revolutionary developments that changed our world.

It is the very basis upon which our most successful social, business, artistic and scientific endeavors have been based.

PERSONAL PERSPECTIVES

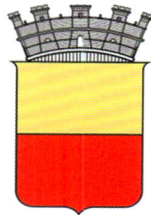

The piazza is a culture, not just real estate.

These are true stories of the piazza…

Barbara's Florence - Piazza della Repubblica

"A Beautiful Experience In the Piazza della Repubblica"

"I'm particularly attached to the Piazza della Repubblica because of many beautiful experiences that have spontaneously happened to me there.

I meet my foreign clients there to start their tour of Florence. It has also always been the meeting place with my American friend Barry, who has hired me many times to give a tour of the city for his special friends and guests.

One day I had a 1PM appointment with him at Piazza della Repubblica to give a tour to a friend of his who had just arrived from California. It was a sunny day and the square was filled up with people who were having a lunch break in one of the coffee shops before going back to work.

Barbara's Florence - Piazza della Repubblica

There were many tourists passing through it too, since it was a warm springtime afternoon. A fantastic soprano was performing opera arias in the middle of the square, Her amazing voice had drawn a lot of people to gather around her, transfixed by the beauty of her singing.

Since many tourist guides also meet their clients in front of the Savoy Hotel, which is right on the piazza, it has become a meeting place for us too. As I was standing there, talking to a colleague of mine, I saw Barry walking towards me. A second later my attention focused on the lady who was with him, his friend. She was wearing a long flowery dress and a wide hat to protect her face from the sun. She was walking so elegantly that it looked like she was floating. It was not only her beauty, but even more, the energy that surrounded her, that made her look like she didn't belong this world. She seemed like a vision. After being introduced, our eyes met and I felt something that can only be describe with the word "energy". This "energy" was going from her eyes to deep insid me, as deep as my "anima", my very soul.

Barbara's Florence - Piazza della Repubblica

We all spent a beautiful afternoon enjoying the beauty of my city. This was six years ago and that "angel" felt in love with my city so much that she decided to stay here forever and has become my best friend!!! This is a story of deep friendship and "love", born at first sight on Piazza della Repubblica, a magic place!!!

Love grows in the interaction between people, and the piazzas are the way to be together, spaces where human emotion, intelligence, friendship and love can blossom."

Barbara's Florence - Piazza Santo Spirito

"When I decide to go out alone or with friends, dressed casually, and I want to feel free, I go to Piazza Santo Spirito. There is a relaxed atmosphere even when the square is filled up with people. I always see somebody I know and, in the process, I'm often introduced to new people. Through this dynamic, my circle of friends is constantly growing. There is no dress code, there is no need to show off. We don't feel either rich or poor, elegant or casual, sophisticated or hippie... we just feel ourselves: Florentines.

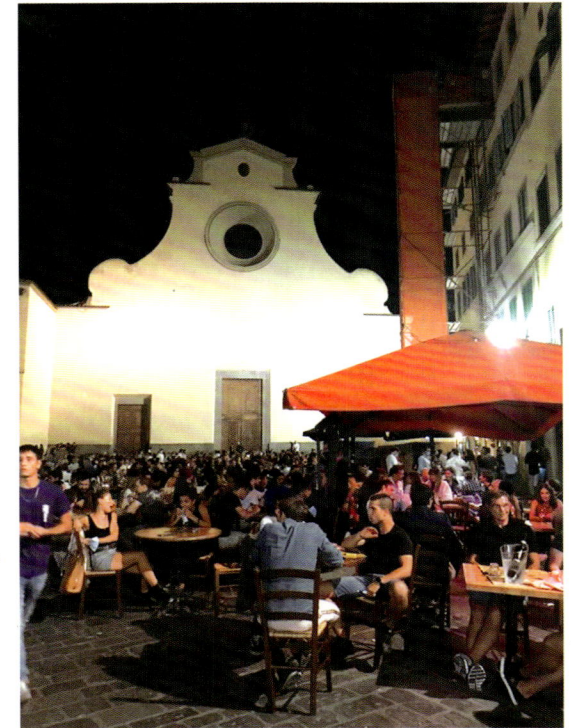

In Piazza Santo Spirito we lose the consciousness that Florence is a touristy city which we share with the world. Here we feel it's only ours and we become more provincial, less cosmopolitan. There is a sense of pride that we can read in people's faces. After all, we were for a long period during the Renaissance, the political, cultural and economic center of the Western world.

The Piazza Santo Spirito was first included within the medieval walls of Florence in the Twelfth Century. While not as old as Piazza della Repubblica - which dates back to Roman times - the Piazza Santo Spirito was created in medieval times for the faithful to gather in front of the newly-built Agostinian church. The church was associated with early humanism.

Barbara's Florence - Piazza Santo Spirito

Among the district's inhabitants were some of the most prominent and ancient families, alongside working-class people.

The square was not only a religious space, but also a cultural meeting place for the inhabitants of the Oltrarno area of Florence – a district along the South bank of the Arno River inhabited by artisans and craftsmen. Even today, it has never lost the atmosphere of an artistic enclave.

Today the Oltrarno is closed off, protected from traffic and mass tourism. It experiences extremes in both economic range and cultural sophistication. It maintains a profound dignity, an energetic expression, an ancient popular wisdom, an ever-present consciousness of its own traditions, along with a provoking spirit of independence. These are the characteristics of the inhabitants of the narrow streets, in the middle of which extends the brightly lit Piazza Santo Spirito, dominated by the elegant and original facade of the church. To this day, it is still an important meeting point for the district's population. There is a daily lively market where local people go shopping. The several trattorias and cafes within this area are traditional - their menus still only written in Italian, and they are filled with Florentines at lunchtime. Even prices are lower than in the center, because it's less touristy. Only the foreigners who travel to experience the real culture of the places they visit are to be seen admiring the church, visiting authentic craft workshops or exploring the narrow streets nearby. The square, with its fountain, is lined with ancient palaces that once belonged to noble and rich merchant families.

Barbara's Florence - Piazza Santo Spirito

The church and the trattorias embody the idea of the real authentic Italian piazza. This piazza is less 'international', less 'bourgeois' than Piazza della Repubblica. People who are seen there are there because they live nearby and they know they can meet an acquaintance, even while just buying their morning newspaper at the news stand.

The stairs in front of the church are always filled up with teenagers who sit there on a sunny day just to talk and watch people. In the evening, Florentines from other parts of the city go to Piazza Santo Spirito to have a drink and feel free in such an intimate neighborhood space. Teenagers, artists, bohemians, hippies, intellectuals – they all love the place. It's not a "Salotto" with elegant sofas in the cafes, it's rustic, and the most sought-after seats are the stairs of the church and the edges of the fountain.

Right after the first COVID lock-down ended in May of 2020, I went to Piazza Santo Spirito to meet a friend who lives in the neighborhood nearby. That's what I had missed for a month and a half... my city!!! Being forced to stay at home, without being able to go downtown and admire Brunelleschi's dome was like killing our souls. But, not being able to go to a piazza like Piazza Santo Spirito for a coffee with a friend, and not have that feeling of belonging to the same city we all love so much, it was like losing our identity."

Barbara's Florence - Piazza della Cure

"If Piazza della Repubblica is the 'Salotto Buono' (the great living room of the city), everybody's meeting place for a coffee, or the starting point for shopping in town, it's also an obligatory stop for the tourists that visit Florence… And, Piazza Santo Spirito is the Oltrarno District's square where all Florentines, not just the neighborhood inhabitants, feel that they belong to the same historic and cultural background. Piazza delle Cure is a square outside the city center and it's neither for the tourists nor for all Florentines, it's just for the people who live in its neighborhood.

It's not an historic place, since it only dates back to the 19th century and it takes its name from the "curandaie", the washerwomen that used to wash the linen cloth in the Mugnone River nearby. I have been living in this area for 54 years and I love it. It's an area where you smell the old city (15 minute walk) and the beautiful countryside, (10 minute drive from the Fiesole hill) at the same time. It doesn't have fashionable shops as in the city center, but it does have everything you might need.

The 'Farmacia della Nave' is one of the most well-stocked pharmacies, and I go there almost every day to buy something. There is the famous Gelateria Cavini, where you see people you know sitting outside to enjoy an ice cream cone anytime of the year. There are several trattorias, a paint shop that sells everything you might need, and the hairdresser 'Achille' who knows exactly each of his clients' hair color number by heart. But the most important meeting place is the cartoleria (stationary store).

Barbara's Florence - Piazza della Cure

Since there are five schools in the neighborhood, from kindergarten to middle school, we mothers all meet there to buy our children stuff for school. And, you can be sure that it always has everything we need, even the most absurd items. Why? Because the two owners buy according to what the teachers and professors of the several schools ask the students to buy. For instance, last year my 15-year old daughter had a crazy professor of technology who asked them to buy specialized equipment that not even a university student of architecture might need!

Last September, I remember going there every day for a whole week to buy special adhesive scotch tape, pencil tips, etc. - for a total of 100 Euros. Groups of mums gathered outside the shop to complain about the teacher, how much money we had to spend for his subject, and much more. It was an occasion to meet and talk about that, and many other things as well. The owners of the shop knew everything about that teacher, as they do about any other teacher of the "Istituto Comprensivo delle Cure".

Our children love to go to the public garden and to the church nearby, but what they enjoy the most are the 99-cent shops in the piazza. They go there to buy so much junk they can afford by themselves, for cheap presents, etc. Anytime our teenage girls meet to go to Piazza delle Cure, we mums can be sure to see them coming back super happy with a bag of junk from those stores.

Barbara's Florence - Piazza della Cure

Two years ago the square was completely renovated: new parking places and sidewalks were added because of too much traffic. We were all desperate, especially because the daily market was moved somewhere else for a year and a half. The market is the real focus point for us inhabitants of the quartiere. It contains many stands that sell everything from food to clothes.

One day, I was buying some Christmas decorations there, when I heard my name. I turned around and there she was: Maria. Maria is the friend I grew up with - she lived 500 meters from my house and we were always together from the age of 3 to the age of 18. Same schools, same friends. I used to drive her on my little scooter from the age of 14, no helmet back then!!!

Maria met an American guy, whom she later married and then moved outside the city. I hadn't seen her in a long time. That day she had come to visit her parents who still live near my house and, of course, she had decided to go shopping in the market in Piazza delle Cure. It was the warmest embrace I can remember. It had been many years without seeing each other, but it felt like 'yesterday' - the time we were teenagers together. Too much to talk about, so we decided from that morning to see each other each time she comes into Florence to see her parents so that we can talk about our lives 'in episodes'. And that's what we have been doing so far!!!

Piazza delle Cure is our piazza only, nobody else is allowed there!!! It's for us who go to the same church, for us whose children go to the same schools, it's for us who have used the same hairdresser for years, it's for us who have the same family doctor in the clinic one block from the

Barbara's Florence - Piazza della Cure

piazza. It's part of the daily routine to go to Piazza della Cure for us, and not only when we want to meet people or go shopping on a free day. There is always a specific 'need' when we go there (buy something, go to the doctor's...) but we can never plan how much time it will take, because the 'need' turns into the "pleasure" to stop to talk to people who share with us the idea of belonging, not so much to the same historic background, but to the same living part of the world."

Barbara Bartolozzi is a native Florentine and a gifted tour guide,who brings her city's past to life through her extraordinary mind and heart. Her love and passion for the city of Florence, and her understanding of its history and art, have been a real gift to me on my journey of understanding the deeper origins of the Renaissance.

Mary's Story - A Therapist's Perspective

"The Arcetri Piazza has the potential to be a central construct of our healing. It is the place where the experience of being human is revived, revitalized and enlivened.

This genius design of intimate, open-air town centers is the ancient remedy for a modern affliction. Instead of driving your car to go to a big box store or a closed-in retail-centered mall, imagine walking out of your house and down the street to hear music, enjoy a coffee, go to the market, and gather with your friends. Experience the joy of the spontaneous interaction that has the power to revive the sense of connection, and bring light to the darkness of loneliness.

Long before the pandemic, the impact of disconnection was seen and felt all around us. I am speaking here of relational human connection.

Mary's Story - A Therapist's Perspective

As a social worker and psychotherapist for teen girls and young women, I have seen physical and psychological evidence of this suffering. For more than seventeen years, I have been witness to the loss of self that results when people lose contact with other people.

The Arcetri Piazza is a common space that can bring one back to being human because it offers a contextual basis for relationship that is easy, natural, and grounded. The Arcetri Piazza is a place to take care of daily needs while having fun and experiencing the simple joy of being together. Eating. Dancing. Talking. Connecting. Shopping for groceries. Living together, in the flow of being human. It is these fundamental experiences that can serve as the antidote to the commodification of people and free us from the captivation of technology and the marketplace.

Mary's Story - A Therapist's Perspective

When the energy of the connection between people gets displaced into a material-based economy, the value of love and the value of togetherness gets down-graded in favor of designer fashion, status, and 'likes' on social media. It also plays out in a core hunger to be seen, felt, and understood. Quite literally, we are starved for love, affection, and connection. We have become neurotically focused on food, physical attractiveness, and material things. A significant part of our economy consists of industries that are organized around cultivating our insecurity, bringing our attention to what we lack. And convincing us that the way to solve the problem is by purchasing whatever product or service is being peddled.

Clearly we are discussing principles that suggest a need for change on a fundamental basis. And when we hear 'change' we get scared because we assume that change will be painful. This change is different. This change is delightful! And charming! With human-centric design, the built environment has the power to help us remember what we have lost.

43

Mary's Story - A Therapist's Perspective

Even though we have mostly forgotten the basic joys of being connected to each other, we are still defined by our deepest core longing: the wish to be loved. Not 'liked' on Facebook. Loved. Known. Seen. The essence of our being has not forgotten our core need, and it is in a communal space, enlivened with the energy that comes from people sharing simple, daily, routine experiences that we can begin to heal."

Mary Waldon, LCSW
Mary Waldon is a graduate of the University of Chicago's School of Social Service Administration and the clinical social work internship at Northwestern Memorial Hospital. She specializes in work with teenage girls and young adult women.

Luca's Naples - The Piazza Was My Life

"I first became part of the scene at Piazza Bellini when I was 14 years old. Each evening, I began to travel with my brothers to the piazza, and that's where I learned so many things.

Over the countless evenings I spent there with my group of friends, we became a kind of Piazza family: an extension to my birth family. It was a small, very intimate group, and with them I grew up. Every night, it was a different fun life.

Over time we moved to a different piazza. Every minute of almost every day we were helping each other, you were never alone, and we found adventure in just being together.

We lived in the moment, yet we were aware we would have to have a future. My father was a professional jazz musician and I was in a rock band. Over time, I looked to find work that was more stable and so I studied hair styling and was already working at it from the age of 15.

45

Luca's Naples - The Piazza Was My Life

At the age of 20, I left for England in search of greater opportunity, and then five years later, I landed in Miami and discovered this wonderful country.

Since coming to America, I have had the opportunity to build a great career with lots of recognition for my abilities, along with gaining financial success.

Napoli and its piazza lifestyle gave me the passion to pursue what I loved, and this passion continued even today as I style and color hair professionally and, along the way, I have made many wonderful acquaintances.

Luca's Naples - The Piazza Was My Life

My hope for the future is that someday I get back that daily feeling of connection and friendship that I enjoyed in the piazza: to regain that openness of the heart that is not touched by other considerations.

I have learned that everything here you have to pay for. It's a rat race. Along the way, while I gained success, I lost everything that mattered to me."

Gianluca Castaldo is an award-winning hairstylist in Miami, Florida.
He founded his wildly successful Bleach Hair Addict salon in 2012.

47

Barry's Story - The Tyrolean Factor

"In 1990, I was asked to host two South Tyrolean mountain men who were visiting Los Angeles. At one point, while I was at home in Malibu, I looked out the window and saw the mountain men sitting quietly on a stone fence. Nearly an hour later I looked again, and they had hardly moved. I asked my friend, 'What are they doing?' She laughed and said, 'They're enjoying nature.' It was pretty much the first time in my life I had ever seen an adult sit still, quite content to be doing nothing. Not reading, watching TV, working, talking, moving or rushing around. Just sitting there, enjoying nature.

The Alps

Malibu

While these two men seemed to be the classic image of 'Mountain Men Farmers' with unruly beards, large calloused hands and workman–like clothes, I soon learned that they were well-educated, worldly and sophisticated. They had a kind of innate, acute intuitive intelligence.

Barry's Story - The Tyrolean Factor

A few years later, inspired by my initial meeting with the two Tyrolean mountain men, I journeyed to the mountainous Merano locale of Italy where I spent a month seeing what this region was all about. What started out as an extended vacation soon became a personal research project leading to a revelation.

Merano, South Tyrol

This semi-autonomous region (state) in Italy is known as South Tyrol (or, as the Italians call it, Alto Adige). It is a very special place with wonderful people. Up until 1919, it had long been part of the Austro-Hungarian Empire. It was there in the South Tyrol that I came to really understand the power of human interaction. I went there to find out what made these people so special. As the weeks went by, I first thought the reason might be the combination of wonderfully clean air and water, along with their excellent diet. Then, as more time went by, I thought it was because of the small, homogeneous population.

49

Barry's Story - The Tyrolean Factor

But, in the end, nothing seemed to provide an adequate explanation of the simpatico nature and overall happiness of these people. I finally gave up trying to understand where these qualites came from.

As we were departing for a drive to Brussels, something unusual happened. This was in the days before the widespread use of GPS, and we were unsure of the best route. On the way out of town, we stopped near a church to ask someone for directions. Before I knew it, the map was spread out across the hood of our car and eight people who had just left the Sunday morning service were discussing the best possible routing until finally, one person exclaimed, 'Go get so and so - she used to live in Brussels.' Someone found the woman and brought her back to our car. She, of course, knew the best route and we were soon on our way.

These local people used this minor crisis to come together as group to find a solution. The feeling was intense, uplifting and full of joy. Today, we have the almost magical technology of GPS, which everyone now uses on their phones and in their cars, without a thought. Yet, as a result of this, we have one less reason to interact with others. And, it is one less skill (sense of direction) that we no longer need in order to get by in the world.

Barry's Story - The Tyrolean Factor

With all this technological progress, the simple act of pausing for the pure joy of sharing, being together and helping one another still matters."

Barry B. Scherr

Mr. Scherr is a life-long commercial real estate innovator and a certified instructor of the Transcendental Meditation™ Technique. He is the author of this book, as well as the 2017 book "Enlightened Real Estate".

How a Piazza Lifestyle & a Train Can Transform a Community
Michael's Culver City Experience

"What gives a place a positive feeling or 'energy'? What makes people want to spend time there? How does a community become more vital? I have been fortunate to have lived in a communi where a transformation like this was taking place.

In 2001, my wife and I moved to Culver City, California, which is a small city within the greater Los Angeles area. At that time, Culver City was a modest community with an underutilized downtown. Many artists and musicians had been moving to Culver City drawn by the lower housing costs. Up to then, Culver City's major claim to fame was that it had been the location for movie sound stages going back to the early days of Hollywood.

How a Piazza Lifestyle & a Train Can Transform a Community
Michael's Culver City Experience

Within a few years, the Culver City city council decided to revitalize the downtown area. They revised their zoning rules to make it easier for new restaurants and retail stores to open. A new movie theater complex was built right across from the famous-but-run-down Culver Hotel. An intersection was relocated to allow the building of a plaza area between the hotel, theater and adjoining restaurants. Within a couple of years, several very good restaurants began appearing in the downtown area, along with a new multi-story retail and parking complex that was within easy walking distance from the central plaza/theater area.

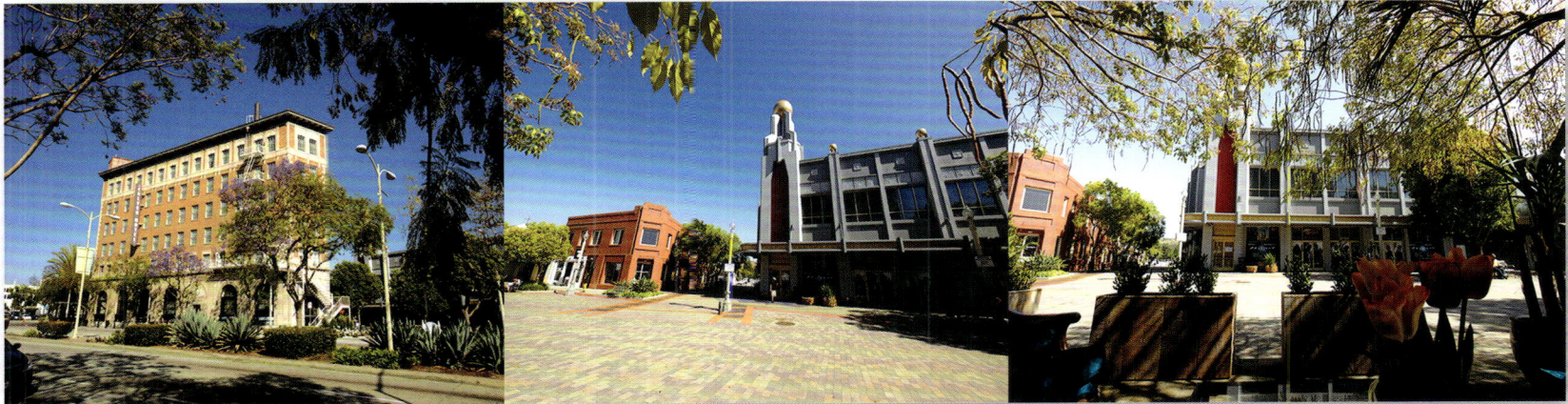

Culver City began gained a reputation as an attractive place to live, as well as a desirable entertainment destination, with a walkable downtown area and plenty of free or inexpensive parking nearby.

How a Piazza Lifestyle & a Train Can Transform a Community

Michael's Culver City Experience

Many art galleries began relocating to West Washington Blvd. – about a ½ mile east of downtown Culver City. This area was anchored by the Helms Bakery complex – a large tract of industrial buildings that once housed a large commercial bakery, but since then has been revitalized with the arrival of numerous good restaurants, along with photography and artist's studios. Culver City designated East Culver City as the 'Arts District'. Suddenly every weekend was mobbed with people walking up and down Washington Blvd., enjoying the galleries, wine shops, coffee bars and restaurants.

Then Los Angeles County made the decision to run its new Metro light rail system from downtown LA to the beach at Santa Monica, with two stops in Culver City.

BEING TOGETHER

THE REBIRTH OF THE PIAZZA

How a Piazza Lifestyle & a Train Can Transform a Community
Michael's Culver City Experience

The piazza-like space between Culver Hotel and the theaters & restaurants connected the local community and created a local identity with added convenience, and the train expanded that experience to the wider urban landscape. The piazza/train experience transformed a sleepy downtown area into a thriving, exciting destination. This is a sound formula for revitalizing a modern urban or suburban environment. This approach uses much less energy and is more practical and convenient than the standard commercial development that is in some cases now struggling to survive. Adding an Arcetri Piazza with additional transit options can boost the popularity and success of any suburban or urban center."

Michael's Venice

"Over the years, I have had the good fortune of spending time in the magical city of Venezia – the Queen of the Adriatic. It began with a month-long shoot for a film I made about glass artist Dale Chihuly, and then continued for many years thereafter, as my wife and I returned to Venice so that she could continue her apprenticeship with a Murano glass bead-making maestro.

As time passed, we made friends with a number of local Venezianos and enjoyed many family and friend gatherings there. Piazzas (or 'campos' as most piazzas are called in Venice) often served as the setting for these get-togethers.

Our first serious Venice friendship occurred in the course of my filming near an antique shop located in Campo San Maurizio. This small campo, dominated by the Chiesa (church) di San Maurizio, is often the site of popular outdoor antique and book markets. We became close friends with the owner of the antique shop: Giulia – a young Veneziana in her early 20's, and then with her extended family. This friendship developed over the years and continues to this day. We enjoyed meals in cafes situated in

56

Michael's Venice

nearby Campo San Stefano. We watched families relaxing on the campo. The air was filled with the sounds of children playing, mixed-in with the pleasant hum of Italian chatter between locals. This was punctuated by the occasional ringing of church bells, along with the echoing, burbling sounds of passing vaporettos and water-taxis. It is the symphony of life in Venice.

One memorable day, as we were walking from our apartment to meet with friends in Campo San Stefano, we encountered a young woman playing beautiful Vivaldi violin solos in the middle of Campo San Maurizio. She was playing her heart out, those healing sounds echoing off the ancient buildings making up the borders of the small campo.

Here in these campos, we often met friends from the States who were passing through Venice and had time only for a cup of coffee. We met friends of friends and extended our web of connections with each passing year. These ancient, wonderful public spaces really do function like an extension of everyone's home – a communal living room shared by friends, strangers, children, the elderly, tourists and locals alike.

57

Michael's Venice

Returning to the States has always been a bit of an adjustment, since there are no comparable public spaces like the Italian piazzas. In the U.S., meetings are almost always scheduled, leaving little room for spontaneous connections. By contrast, in Italy a normal day often includes a series of unexpected opportunities to enjoy the flow of the human heart."

Michael W. Barnard, MFA
Michael is a filmmaker, photographer, writer, artist and designer.
He assisted Barry with his previous book, "Enlightened Real Estate".
Michael lives and works in Santa Fe, New Mexico.

Regaining the True Joy of Architecture & Building
Barry's Personal Perspective

"Most architects and builders love their profession. They create structures for everyday living at the busy crossroads where beauty, symmetry, harmony, balance, health, happiness, and even enlightenment intersect.

Buildings provide the backdrop for the theater of life.

I've always loved to work, but when I began to work less, I discovered the joy of walking through intimate Italian streets past an endless parade of ancient buildings built for the scale of humans, not cars.

59

BEING TOGETHER

THE REBIRTH OF THE PIAZZA

Regaining the True Joy of Architecture & Building

When I returned to America, again and again I was faced with the realization that we had lost much of the serendipity and gracefulness of life. We have to plan everything here, since we don't have common spaces which allow us to spontaneously run into one another in the course of daily living. What should be a leisurely, human-centric schedule has turned into an exhausting rush to try and fit-in each activity and meeting. The memory of the joy of being together fades and it seems logical for us to do things one at a time: work, exercise, friends, family – each siloed in their own time and place, with too much driving in-between. We've accepted inconvenience as the new normal"

This is the story of remembering how to establish a graceful, healthy lifestyle...

PICTURE GALLERY

DOUBLE PAGE PHOTOS

1.) CAMPO SAN STEFANO - VENICE
2.) CAMPO SAN STEFANO - VENICE
3.) PIAZZA DELLA REPUBBLICA - FLORENCE
4.) PIAZZA DELLA REPUBBLICA - FLORENCE
5.) MARKET - FLORENCE
6.) POSITANO
7.) FORTE DEI MARMI
8.) ARCETRI PIAZZA RENDERING

SINGLE PAGE PHOTOS

1.) LUCCA
2.) PIAZZA DELLA SIGNORIA- FLORENCE
3.) VIA DEL PONTE VECCHIO - FLORENCE
4.) FLORENCE IN THE RAIN
5.) VIEW OF FLORENCE
6.) TREVI FOUNTAIN - ROME
7.) CAMPO SAN STEFANO - VENICE
8.) POSITANO
9.) LUCCA
10.) CAFE GILLI - PIAZZA DELLA REPUBBLICA - FLORENCE

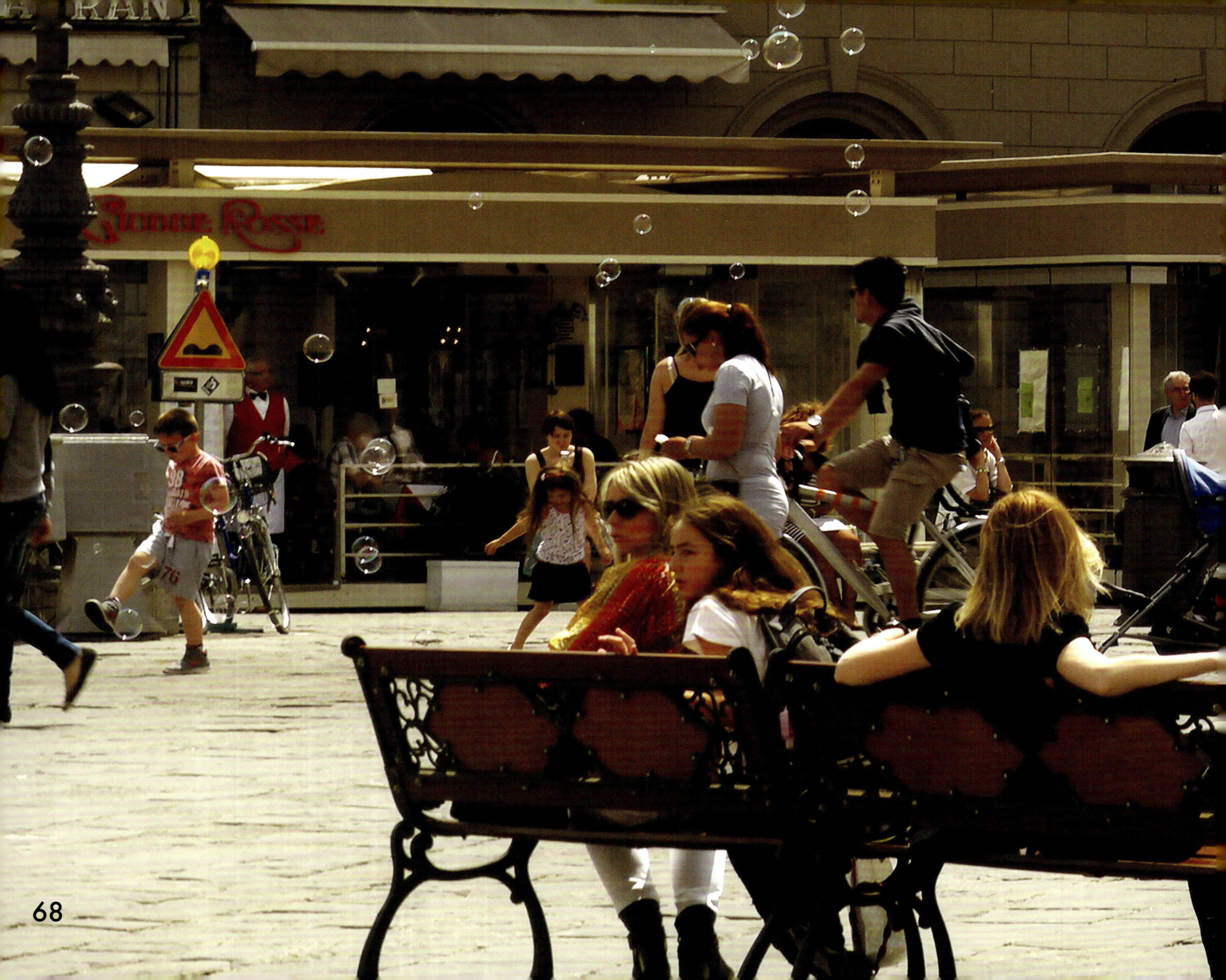
Giubbe Rosse

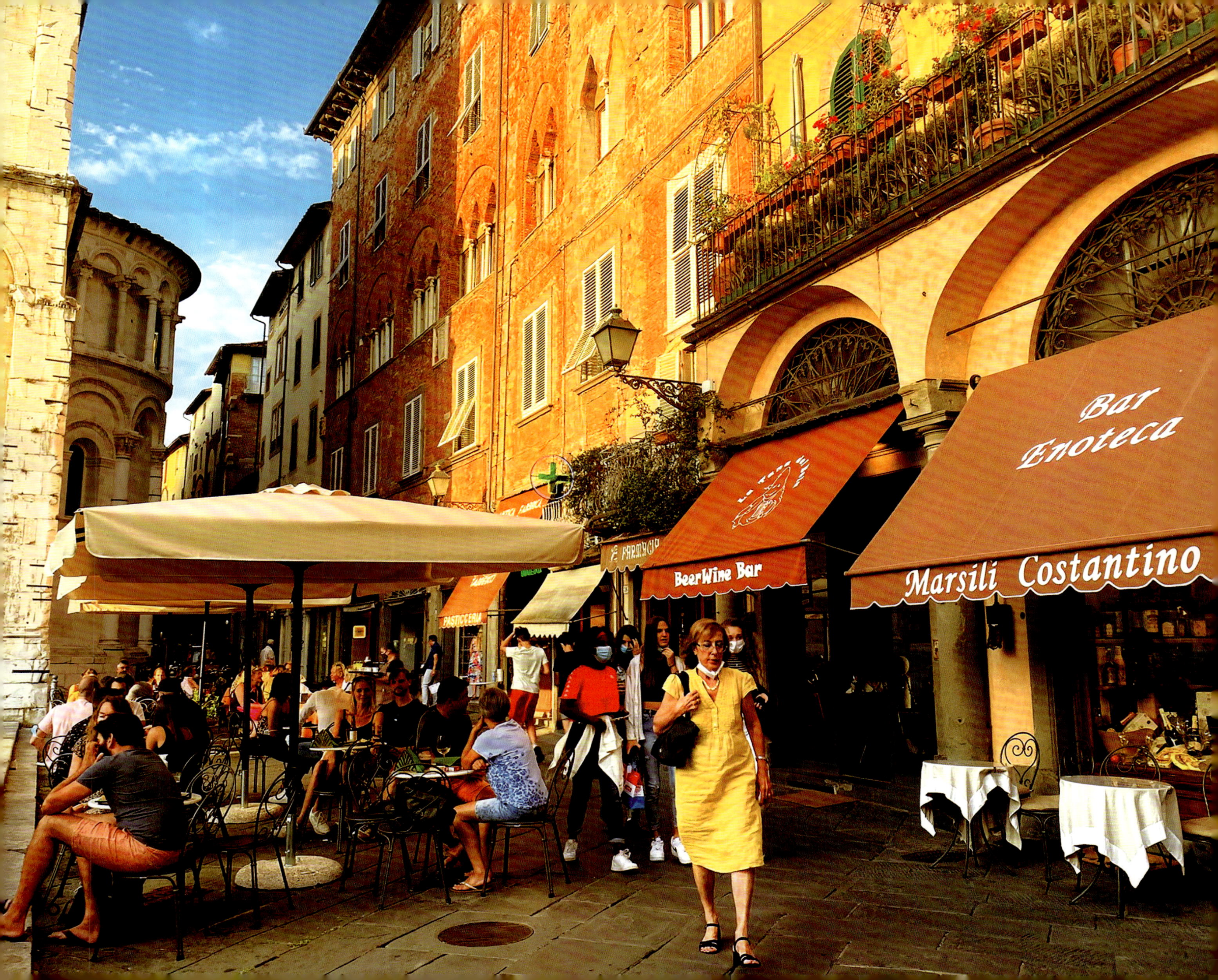
Bar
Enoteca
Marsili Costantino
BeerWine Bar
PASTICCERIA

PART TWO

THE REBIRTH OF THE PIAZZA
FOR THE 21ST CENTURY

ARCETRI
collection

ARCETRI, LLC

THE REBIRTH OF THE PIAZZA

"The Arcetri Piazza is a technology to re-establish human connection: a people-friendly design for establishing wellness, happiness and higher consciousness - a place where people can rediscover the joy of being together."

PART TWO - INTRODUCTION

IMAGINE A WORLD WHERE:

       Everything you think of is at your fingertips,

       There's a beautiful space to gather and share,

       Being together, eating together, growing together is easy and natural,

       Everyday life is supported by a higher purpose,

       There is a place where everyone goes to meet, a place that's easy to be part of.

The Arcetri Italian Lifestyle Piazza invites you to celebrate the human journey.

92

THE ARCETRI PHILOSOPHY - A NEW VISION FOR LIFE

Everything about the Arcetri Italian Lifestyle Piazza concept is designed to provide a home for a new, wellness-oriented, conscious lifestyle that is a bridge between the intimacy of the historical, antique city-centers of Italy, modern technological conveniences, and the subjective power of being together.

WHAT IS AN ARCETRI PIAZZA?

The ARCETRI PIAZZA is where everyday living meets health, happiness and enlightenment. This new vision of the piazza lifestyle combines wellness with the daily routine of life and the joy of being part of a community where everybody matters.

In the course of the day, when people meet in the walking, human-scaled environment of the ARCETRI PIAZZA, they can enjoy the benefits of high-velocity interaction. This re-imagined piazza offers almost every convenience at your fingertips. As obstacles melt away, life flows effortlessly, resulting in a new, expanded dimension of everyday living.

The piazza, as a meeting place, a market, a place for leisure, entertainment and wellness. A timeless space for rediscovering the memory of what it feels like to be together.

A SPACE THAT CAN FLOW WITH YOUR DREAMS AND ASPIRATIONS.

WHAT IS AN ARCETRI PIAZZA?

AN ARCETRI PIAZZA IS THE QUANTUM MECHANICAL SOLUTION FOR SUPPORTING MULTI-DIMENSIONAL LEVELS OF HUMAN BEHAVIOR SIMULTANEOUSLY:

- Shopping
- Errands
- Eating Together
- Exercise
- Socialization
- Meeting & Sharing
- Entertainment
- Celebration
- Connection
- Wellness Services
- Integrative & Alternative Medicine
- Consciousness (Meditation, Yoga)

The Arcetri Piazza takes the best elements of European piazzas and incorporates them into a unique lifestyle design that satisfies the needs of contemporary living.

95

WHAT IS AN ARCETRI PIAZZA?

The Arcetri Piazza conserves the most limited commodity in the modern world: time. How? By placing at one's fingertips the ability to accomplish all of life's daily necessities into one beautiful, enjoyable location.

When you save time, it allows for a balanced life - which includes maximum social interaction, evolution, artistic pursuits, and personal development such as meditation, yoga, exercise, healthy nutrition, etc.

Our lives have been dominated by serial activities (one after another) :

- A mall is for shopping
- An office building is for working.
- A freeway is for driving
- A restaurant is for eating
- A gym is for exercising
- A theater is for entertainment

An Arcetri Piazza supports parallel activities.

The Arcetri Piazza redefines commerce by simultaneously facilitating human health, happiness and evolution.

ARCETRI ITALIAN LIFESTYLE PIAZZA™

WHY THE ARCETRI PIAZZA?

When a tsunami comes, first there's silence, then there is nowhere to hide. Today, an overwhelming wave of change is causing massive obsolescence of many existing properties and business models.

The quality of everyday human experience has become a vital aspect of the real estate conversation. The Arcetri Piazza represents a new asset class which can be built in a number of configurations. It offers a revolutionary concept that will be viable over the long term.

The Arcetri Piazza will prove to be the gold standard to bring the real estate world back into alignment with what people want.

WHY THE ARCETRI PIAZZA?

For decades across the U.S.A., and indeed, around the world, malls were the centerpiece of the commercial, automobile-centric age of consumption. The mall will continue to have its place, but in reduced numbers, and with a more expanded vision. The combination of rapidly changing demographics (the rise of the Millennials), the impact of online shopping, and environmental concerns have necessitated the re-imagining of what a mall could and should be.

During the 1990s Big-box Retail completed the process of converting everyday errands and shopping into a generic transactional process. It was more convenient and more economical, but less personal.

The online retail revolution promised to conveniently deliver goods with no social interaction. While this has proved efficient, it has accelerated social isolation. The notion of the communal marketplace as exemplified by the historic Italian piazza has been forgotten. Today, in response to the public's lessening interest in the purely transactional shopping experience, the development community is searching for ways to create new, more exciting destination experiences that will again capture the public's imagination.

Based on years of research and development, we have developed an entirely new asset class - the Arcetri Piazza: a mixed-use solution to the retail and wellness revolution.

WHY THE ARCETRI PIAZZA?

People have repeatedly asked me, "Isn't a mall the same as a piazza?"
The answer is: "Not at all!"

Today there is an urgent need to re-imagine, reconfigure and rebuild our commercial spaces.

The original idea of the shopping mall was as a town center which would serve the wider commercial and social interests of an exploding suburban population. It was intended to be an updated version of the local downtown center where people could meet, have a meal, and accomplish the errands of the day. In short, a place to gather and enjoy all facets of daily life, not just a place to shop.

The earliest proponent of this idea was Austrian-American architect Victor Gruen. The community-friendly design Gruen envisioned, which combined retail shops with everyday services and separated people from automobile traffic, was never fully realized.

WHY THE ARCETRI PIAZZA?

The Arcetri Piazza focuses on enhancing beneficial human interaction and the ease of daily life, as well as establishing the cultural heart of a community. The Arcetri Piazza is the first asset class that addresses all levels of human experience simultaneously.

THE ARCETRI PIAZZA CULTURE™

The personal and social effects of adopting the Arcetri Piazza lifestyle are multiple and far-reaching. These positive enhancements of life take place over time as a person's physiology and psychology are gently healed and refined through the interaction within the profoundly supportive environment of the Arcetri Piazza - a remedy for the rise of social interaction deficit.

The Arcetri Piazza Culture turns anonymity into community and may include:

+ Greater feelings of happiness and less loneliness due to increased multi-generational social interaction.

+ More satisfying and longer-lasting interpersonal relationships due to greater frequency of spontaneous social interactions as part of one's daily routine.

+ A better daily routine due to the convenience of accomplishing one's daily activities, errands, shopping, work, and social events - all in an easily walkable area.

+ A general increase of intelligence and empathy as one interacts with friends and family more often, thus ensuring that we develop enhanced "emotional intelligence", i.e. – the ability to successfully share happiness (and the occasional sorrow) with a widening group of people that are part of one's daily life.

+ The Arcetri Piazza provides a magnificent "third space" where the expanded value of the community is nourished and sustained through providing a "home" for your life outside your family home and workplace.

+ Greater sense of self and higher consciousness through the practice of Transcendental Meditation™ and yoga practice, which can give a direct experience of one's essential self.

+ Providing easily accessible exercise, aerobics and stretching to preserve strength and vitality.

+ Potential greater wealth through the serendipity of intense, spontaneous personal interactions which often enhance and expand one's personal network, thus supporting and encouraging greater flow of opportunity and solutions.

+ The Arcetri Piazza is created through the proper arrangement of correctly-built buildings. This effect is felt in the form of an energizing influence. Buildings in the Arcetri Piazza are built with specific proportions in a scale that resonates with the human physiology. Just as music creates an experience of contentment and harmony, the Arcetri Piazza operates like an orchestra, where the ensemble of instruments produces an overall positive effect.

+ Regular and repeated experiences of beauty as one's eyes are greeted with uplifting design, lots of living greenscapes, flowers and the extensive use of natural materials. This includes the sophisticated, coherent design of the Arcetri Piazza, which creates in every line of sight a scene of harmony and balance.

+ And, finally, the Arcetri Piazza is a memory machine which awakens a greater sensitivity to the importance of life's journey.

THE ARCETRI PIAZZA CULTURE™

The Arcetri Piazza Culture enlivens all these different levels of human experience

1.) Activity – the normal activities needed for daily life.

2.) Celebration - a wide variety of events, markets and concerts.

3.) Emotional - opening our heart.

4.) Communal Vibrancy – humans are communal creatures and we seek one another out. This includes being together, eating together, playing together, even transcending together.

5.) The relationship of the human species to the natural environment.

6.) Story Telling - we are natural storytellers and we use story-telling as a way to structure and understand our existence.and to convey essential teachings.

7.) The Arcetri Piazza continues the grand story of human evolution in concert with nature.

8.) The celebration of our many great geniuses and heroes throughout history.

The Arcetri Piazza Culture enlivens communal vibrancy and brings people together in a joyful way.

THE ARCETRI PIAZZA CULTURE™

The personal and social effects of adopting the Arcetri Piazza lifestyle are multiple and far-reaching. These positive enhancements to life take place over time as a person's physiology and psychology are refined through the interaction with the profoundly supportive and healing environment of the Arcetri Piazza.

THE ARCETRI PIAZZA AND SUSTAINABLE LIVING

Today's climate crisis is forcing a shift in human awareness about the relationship between our species and the natural world. This shift is really about modern society beginning to remember the inherent connection between all things - the complex, living web of life that binds us all together.

Real estate contributes to the ongoing climate crisis on a number of levels. The focus up till now has been mostly on the energy consumption of buildings rather than the context in which they are built. The real estate world has been struggling to recognize the nature of this challenge. Our solution is a new asset-class that takes into account the entire network of physical buildings, transportation, amenities and lifestyle, and will address the climate crisis at a more fundamental level.

How will we accomplish this?

THE ARCETRI PIAZZA AND SUSTAINABLE LIVING

Up till now most of the attention has been on the individual parts - i.e. the buildings, rather than the whole system in which we live. In order to create a more human-centric, environmentally-sound built environment, we need to seriously consider a total re-imagining of urban and suburban city centers for the modern world.

Our inspiration for this new version of the built enviroment is the historic European city center. For centuries, these historic European city centers and their magnificent piazzas have remained a powerful draw for people from around the world. According to David Owen's best-selling book "Green Metropolis", New York City or European city centers use about 1/3 of the energy per capita as compared to the American-style suburban model. This template could resolve the conflict between lifestyle and energy consumption, while at the same time making it possible for everyone to enjoy a more environmentally sound future.

The Arcetri Piazza offers a revolutionary solution that allows us to enjoy a higher quality lifestyle in a cost-effective way, with minimal environmental impact.

THE ARCETRI PIAZZA AND SUSTAINABLE LIVING

To successfully combat climate change will require many solutions. The most successful methods realign with nature instead of trying to use our human will and intelligence to dominate nature. One promising method is the practice of planting trees on a massive scale, a recognized strategy for trapping CO_2 from the atmosphere. Many other useful strategies are being considered for accomplishing the goal of carbon-neutrality.

Each of these Arcetri Piazzas will serve as a new town center around which, over time, a neighborhood identity and a new way of living will naturally develop. These changes can play an important part in solving our climate crisis challenges.

Living, working and enjoying life in the convenient, walkable environment of an Arcetri Piazza is a dynamic, business AND environmentally-friendly solution.

THE ARCETRI PIAZZA AND SUSTAINABLE LIVING

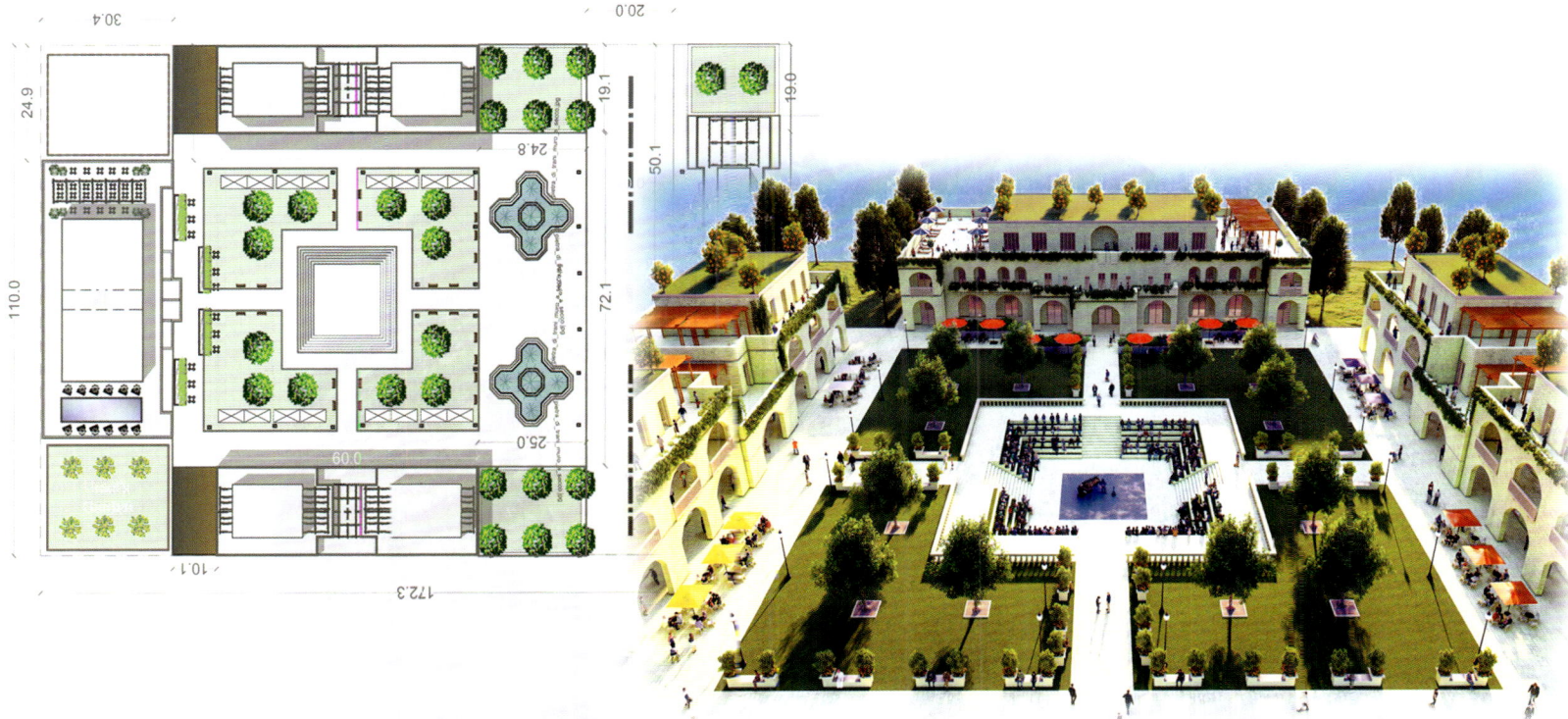

Walking more often through your day, working close to home, doing things you love with people that you enjoy and who care about you: these add-up to a far better lifestyle which is more restful and energizing, while dramatically reducing per-capita emissions and disproving the argument that the earth can only be saved by compromising our quality of life.

The Arcetri Piazza is designed to support the mutually beneficial evolution of Nature and humanity.

THE PIAZZA: PLACE & IDENTITY

The piazza became the heart of the city and public life. Personal feelings, relationships and interaction were naturally renewed in the piazza, and enlivened on a daily basis. Originally built in an age of walking and horses, the overall space of a piazza, and its surrounding streets, have a distinctly human sense of proportion and rightness. These urban spaces were clearly built to serve human needs and support social interaction, daily fresh-food markets, religion and even politics.

Now, in our present-day automobile-centric, transactional culture, we have lost these essentially human experiences, much to the detriment of our physical and emotional well-being.

THE PIAZZA: PLACE & IDENTITY

The piazza is the structure where one can be together in a field of love, friendship and purpose while simultaneously pursuing one's daily routine.

The Formula for the Arcetri Piazza Concept is Revolutionary

By rediscovering the piazza as the center of community life, the Arcetri Piazza establishes a revolutionary new structure that dissolves obstacles to progress, creativity and relationships.

The Arcetri Piazza:

1) Creates curated commercial spaces for the new experiential lifestyles.

2) Utilizes designs that present the beauty and symmetry of the classic Italian piazza.

3) Includes special architectural elements and natural building materials.

4) Encourages multi-generational usage - a safe place for children to play.

THE TEN ARCETRI PIAZZA PROTOTYPES

1.) THE ARCETRI LIFESTYLE PIAZZA
    With an emphasis on Wellness and Everyday Living.

2.) THE ARCETRI GARDEN & EVENT PIAZZA
    Featuring music, art, theater, film and special events.

3.) THE ARCETRI WELLNESS PIAZZA
    Providing the whole wellness world in one location including full health spa services, Pilates, spinning, yoga, Transcendental Meditation, farm-to-table, vegetarian/organic and other healthy food.

4.) THE ARCETRI ENERGY & IDEA PIAZZA
    A mini-Piazza that serves as an ideal creative meeting place.

5.) THE ARCETRI GOLDEN MILLENNIUM PIAZZA
    For young seniors and sophisticated Millennials.

6.) THE ARCETRI ITALIAN EXPERIENCE PIAZZA
    Featuring an authentic Italian Piazza experience for people who love Italy.

7.) THE ARCETRI CORPORATE VILLAGE PIAZZA COMPLEX
  A private Arcteri Piazza that includes offices & supporting amenities
  including corporate dining and guest apartments.

8.) THE ARCETRI PIAZZA AND VILLAGE COMPLEX
    An Ideal Village centered around an Italian-style Arcetri Piazza.

9.) THE ARCETRI PIAZZA EXTENDED FAMILY & FRIENDS COMPOUND
    A private Piazza complex designed to accommodate a multigenerational family.
    (Separate housing with the opportunity to gather in the piazza area.)

10.) THE ARCETRI PIAZZA ENTERTAINMENT COMPLEX
    Featuring a diverse array of entertainment venues and experiences

These Piazza prototypes can be built in a variety of architectural styles.

ARCETRI PIAZZA PROTOTYPE # 1

ARCETRI LIFESTYLE PIAZZA
Architectural Renderings

ARCETRI PIAZZA PROTOTYPE # 1

ARCETRI LIFESTYLE PIAZZA
Architectural Renderings

ARCETRI PIAZZA PROTOTYPE # 1

ARCETRI LIFESTYLE PIAZZA
Architectural Renderings

ARCETRI PIAZZA PROTOTYPE # 1

ARCETRI LIFESTYLE PIAZZA
Architectural Renderings

ARCETRI LIFESTYLE PIAZZA
Architectural Renderings

ARCETRI PIAZZA PROTOTYPE # 2
ARCETRI GARDEN & EVENT PIAZZA
Architectural Renderings

ARCETRI PIAZZA PROTOTYPE # 2

ARCETRI GARDEN & EVENT PIAZZA
Architectural Renderings

ARCETRI PIAZZA PROTOTYPE # 2

ARCETRI GARDEN & EVENT PIAZZA
Architectural Renderings

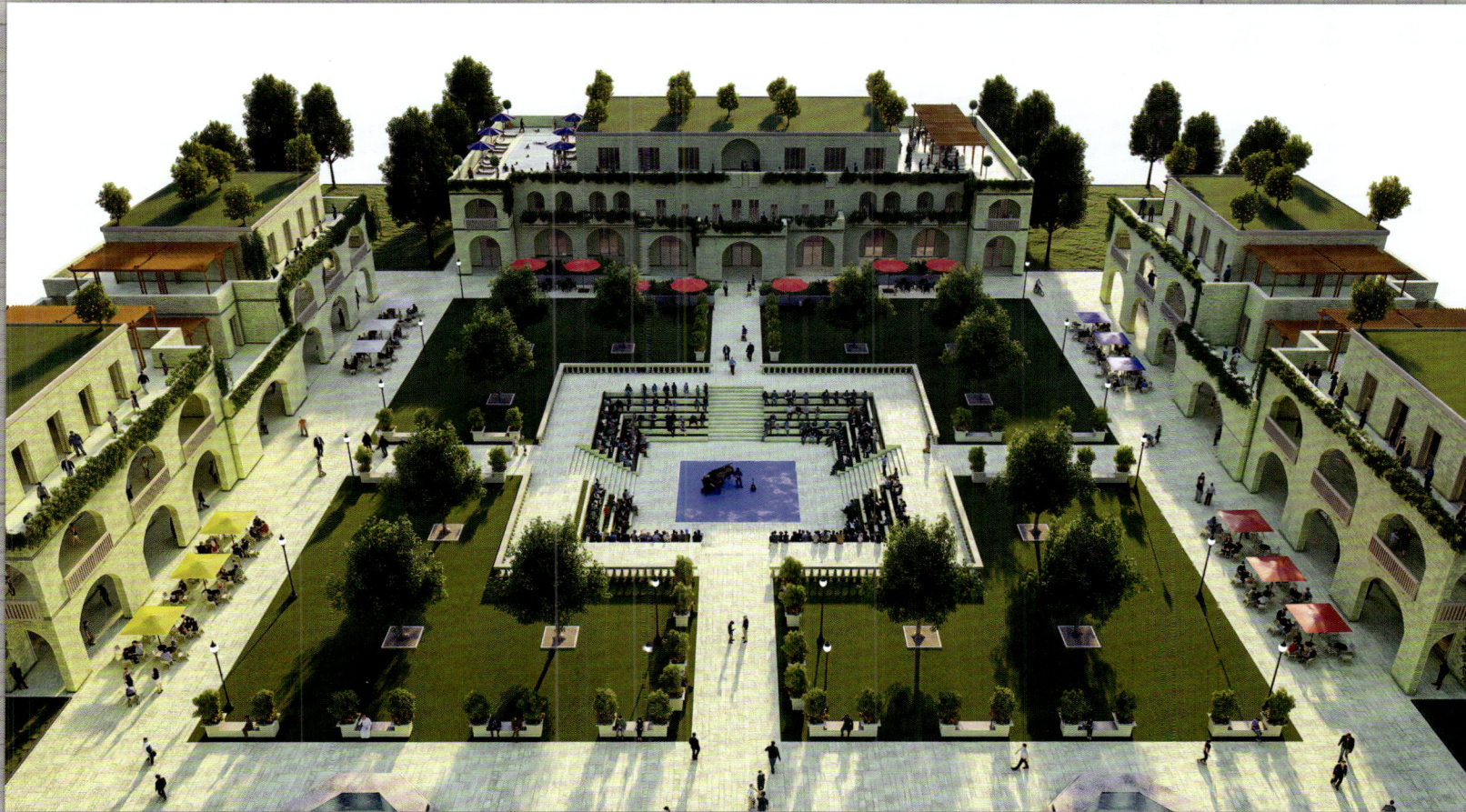

ARCETRI GARDEN & EVENT PIAZZA
Architectural Renderings

ARCETRI PIAZZA PROTOTYPE #1 - LIFESTYLE PIAZZA
Planimetric Development First Floor

BUILDING A:

Area: 18,000 sq. ft.
Volume: 10.800 mc
Use:
Hotel Reception, Services,
Restaurant

BUILDINGS B-C:

Area: 13,000 sq. ft
Volume: 7.800 mc
Use:
Building B - Retail, Restaurants
Building C - Retail, Vegetarian Restaurant

BUILDINGS D-E:

Area: 11,000 sq. ft. x 2 = 22,000 sq. ft.
Volume: 13.200 mc
Use:
Building D - Post Office, UPS service, Bank
Building E - Retail, Computer Store, Vegan Restaurant

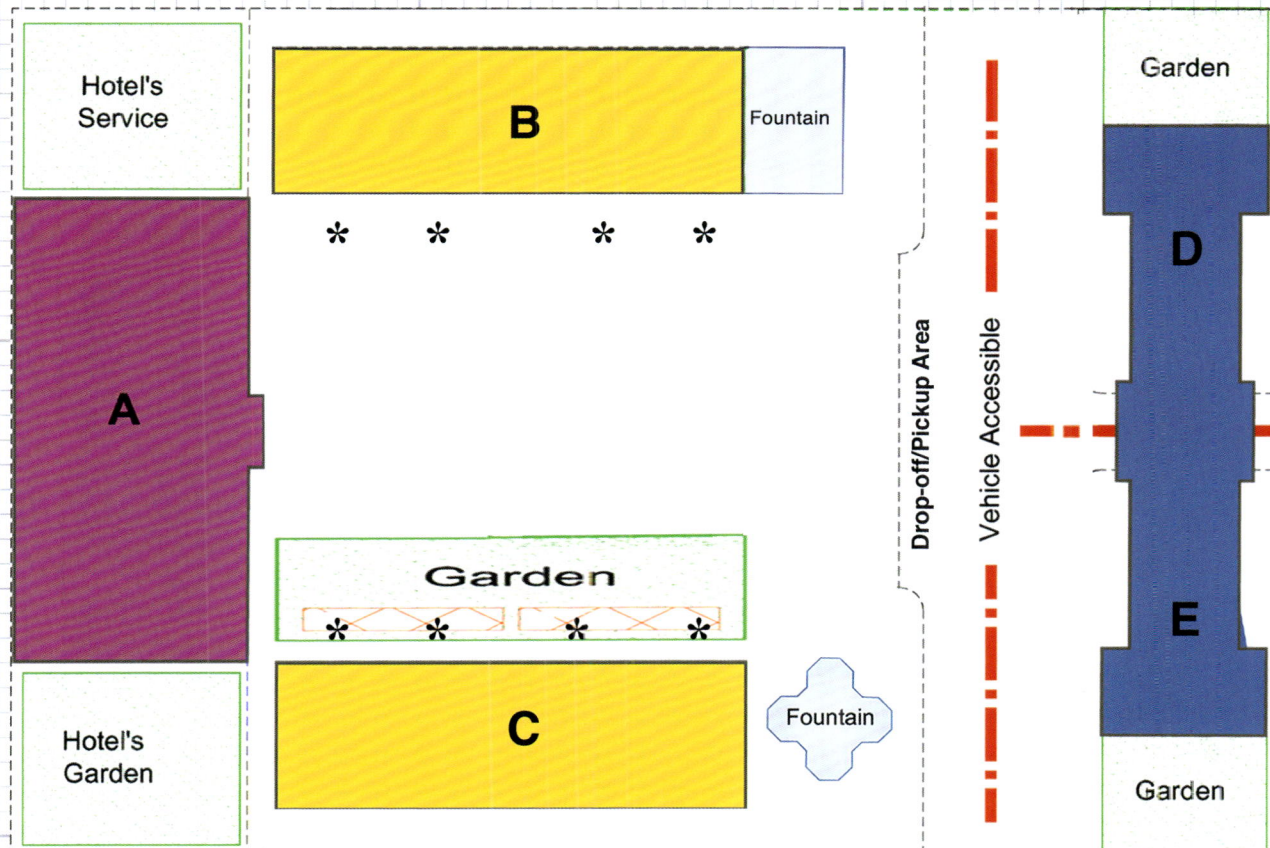

Hotel's Service

B

Fountain

* * * *

A

Garden

Garden

* * * *

Hotel's Garden

C

Fountain

Drop-off/Pickup Area

Vehicle Accessible

Garden

D

E

Garden

*Outdoor Covered Seating

ARCETRI PIAZZA - PROTOTYPE #1 - LIFESTYLE PIAZZA
Planimetric Development Second Floor

BUILDING A:

Area: 17,000 sq. ft.
Volume: 7.225 mc
Use:
Hotel Rooms

BUILDINGS B-C:

Area: 13,000 sq. ft.
Volume: 5.525 mc
Use:
Building B - Offices
Building C - Offices/Apartments

BUILDINGS D-E:

Area: 485 mq x 2 = 9,700 sq. ft.
Volume: 4.130 mc
Use:
Building D - Apartments
Building E - Apartments

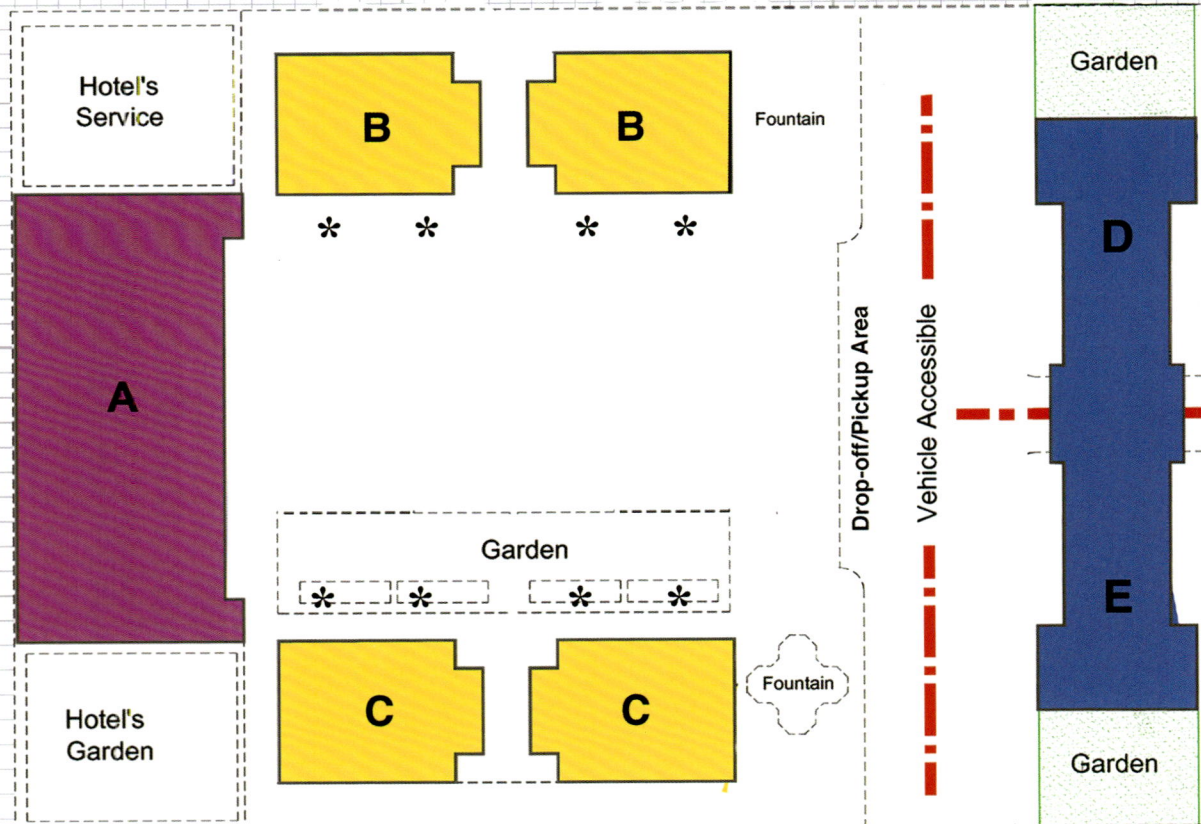

Hotel's Service

B

B

Fountain

*   *   *   *

A

Drop-off/Pickup Area

Vehicle Accessible

Garden

D

Garden

*   *   *   *

C

C

Fountain

E

Garden

Hotel's Garden

*Outdoor Covered Seating

124

ARCETRI PIAZZA PROTOTYPE #1 - LIFESTYLE PIAZZA
Planimetric Development Third Floor - Rooftop Garden

BUILDING A:

Area: 17,000 sq
Volume: 7.225 mc
Use:
Hotel Rooms, Swimming Pool
Roof Garden

BUILDINGS B-C:

Area: 3,700 sq. ft.
Volume: 1.580 mc
Use:
Building B - Apartments
Building C - Apartments

BUILDINGS D-E:

Area: 4,700 sq. ft.
Volume: 2.000 mc
Use:
Building D - Offices/Fitness
Building E - Offices/Apartments

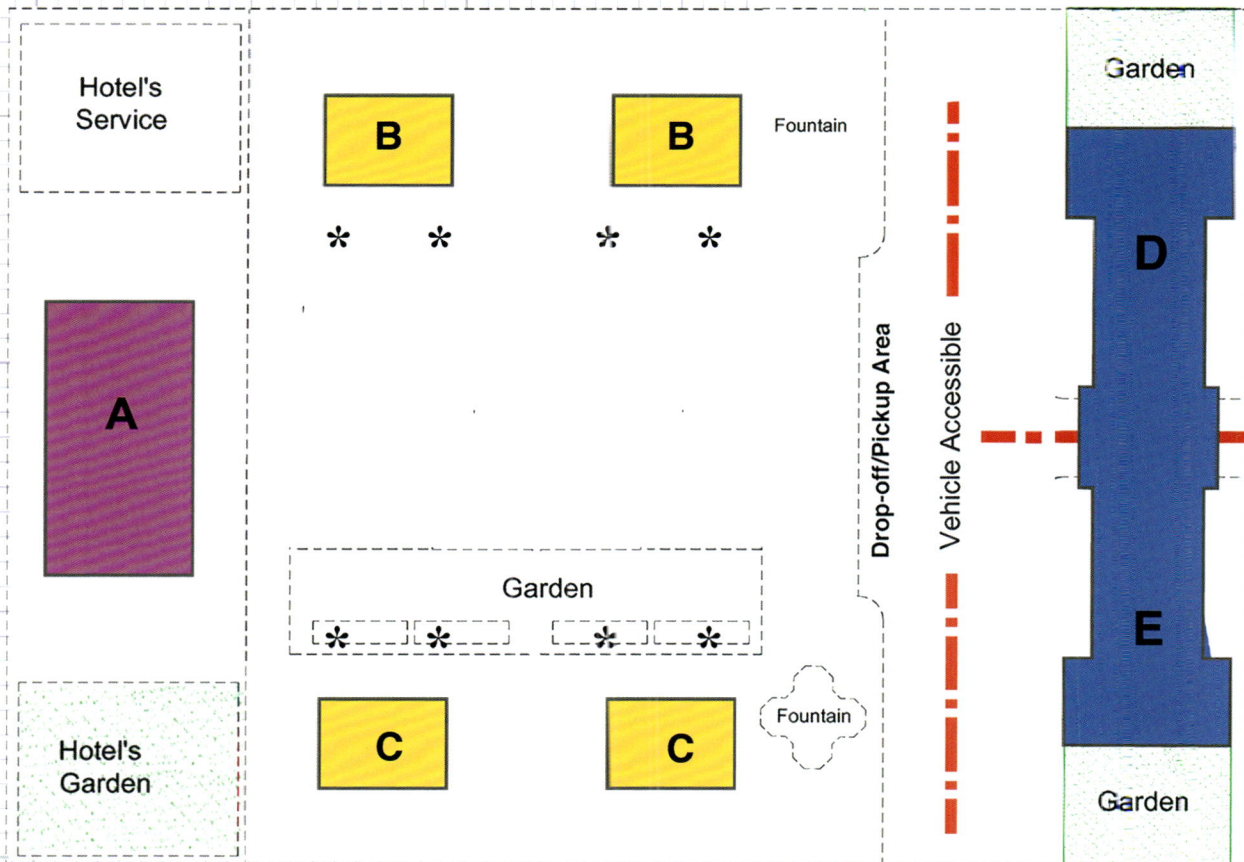

Hotel's
Service

B   B   Fountain

*   *   *   *

A

Garden

*   *   *   *

Garden

D

Drop-off/Pickup Area

Vehicle Accessible

Hotel's
Garden

C   C   Fountain

E

Garden

*Outdoor Covered Seating

125

ARCETRI PIAZZA PROTOTYPE #1 - LIFESTYLE PIAZZA
General Plan of the Area

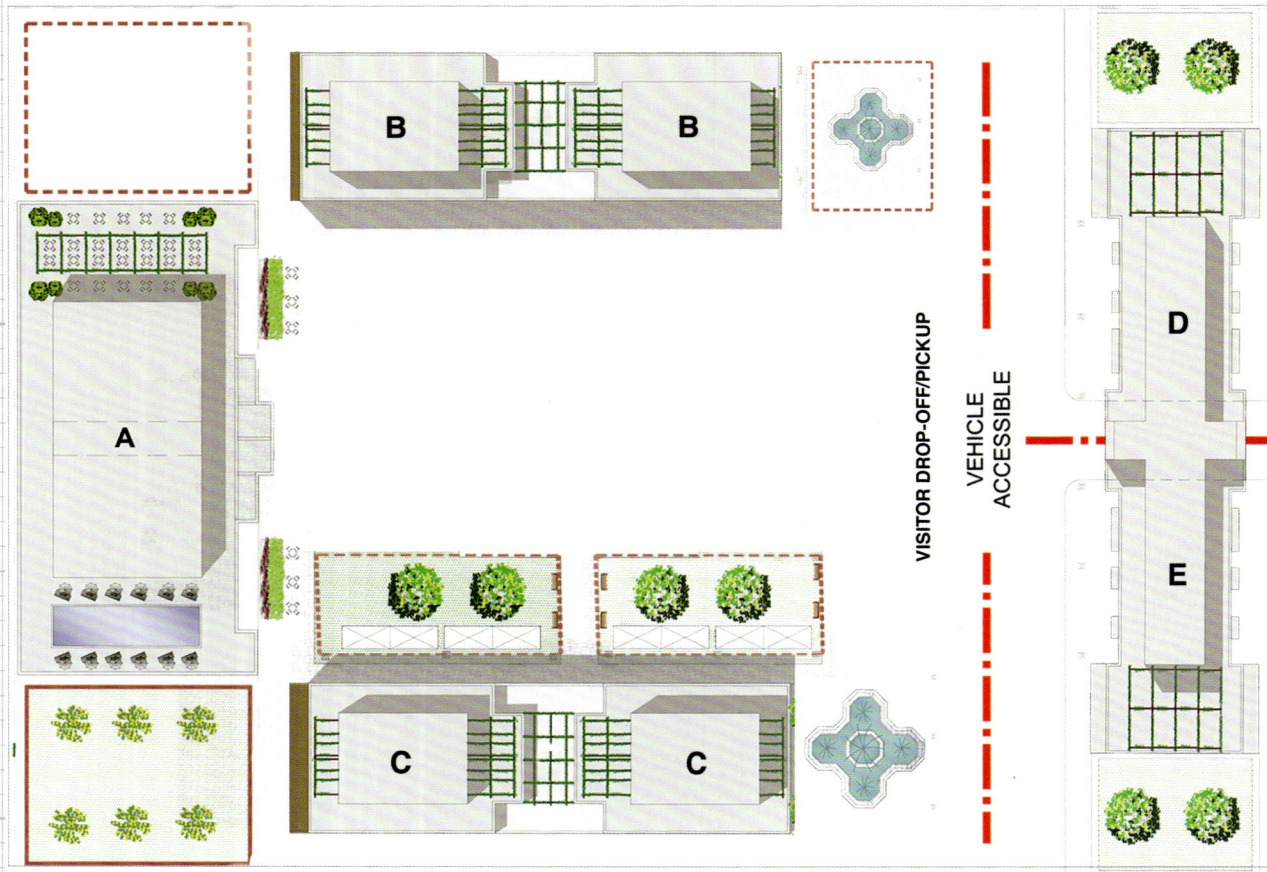

ARCETRI PIAZZA PROTOTYPE #2 - GARDEN & EVENT PIAZZA
Planimetric Development First Floor

BUILDING A:

Area: 18,000 sq. ft.
Volume: 10.800 mc
Use:
Hotel Reception, Services, Restaurant

BUILDINGS B-C:

Area: 13,000 sq. ft.
Volume: 7.800 mc
Use:
Building B - Retail, Restaurants
Building C - Retail, Vegetarian Restaurant

BUILDINGS D-E:

Area: 11,000 sq. ft. x 2 = 22,000 sq. ft.
Volume: 13.200 mc
Use:
Building D- Post Office, UPS service, Bank
Building E - Retail, Computer Store, Vegan Restaurant

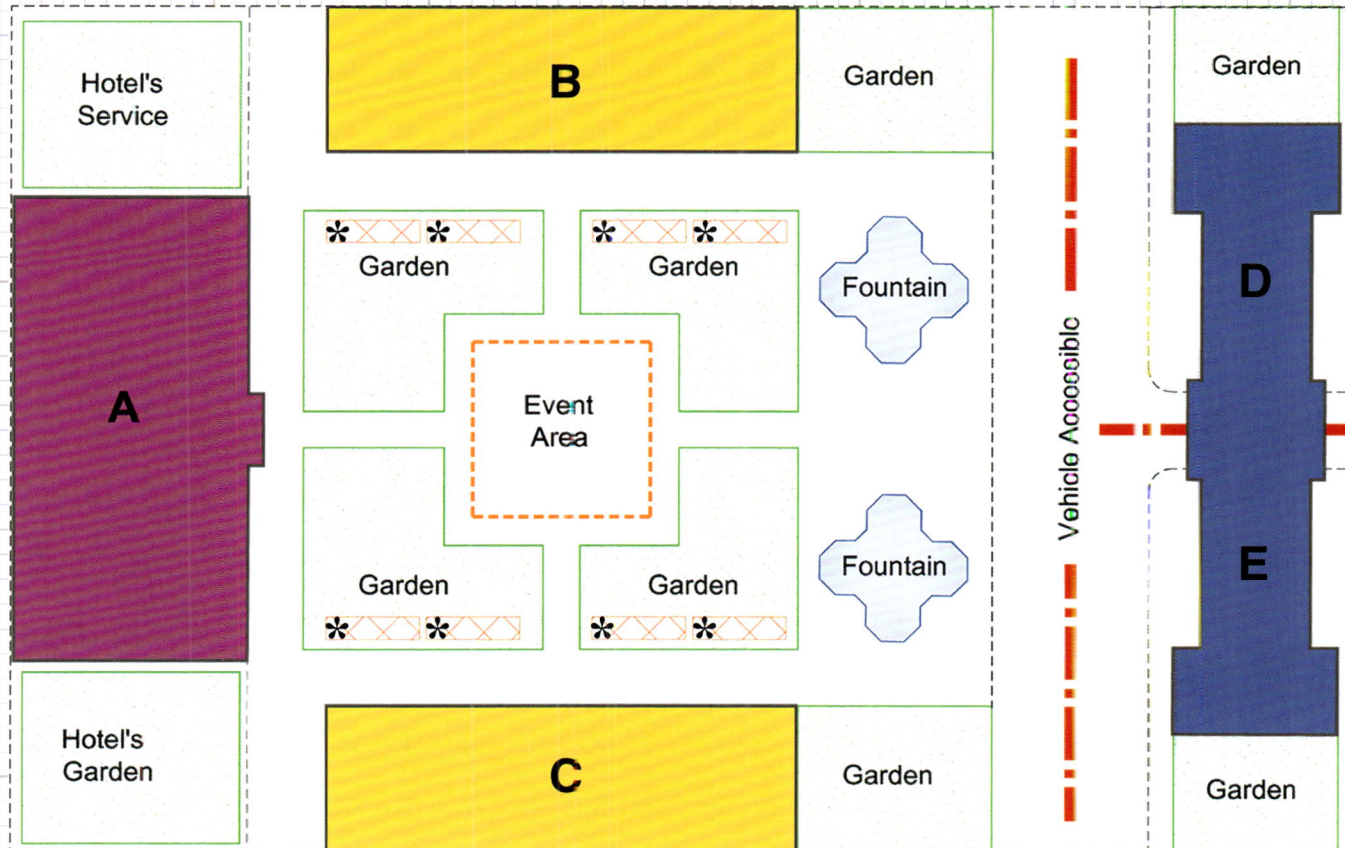

Hotel's Service	**B**	Garden

Garden

* Garden *

* Garden *

Fountain

A

Event Area

Garden

Garden

Fountain

Vehicle Accessible

D

E

Garden

Garden

Hotel's Garden

C

Garden

*Outdoor Covered Seating

ARCETRI PIAZZA PROTOTYPE #2 - GARDEN & EVENT PIAZZA
Planimetric Development Second Floor

BUILDING A:

Area: 17,000 sq. ft.
Volume: 7.225 mc
Use:
Hotel Rooms

BUILDINGS B-C:

Area: 13,000 sq. ft.
Volume: 5.525 mc
Use:
Building B - Offices
Building C - Offices/Apartments

BUILDINGS D-E:

Area: 485 mq x 2 = 9,700 sq. ft.
Volume: 4.130 mc
Use:
Building D - Apartments
Building E - Apartments

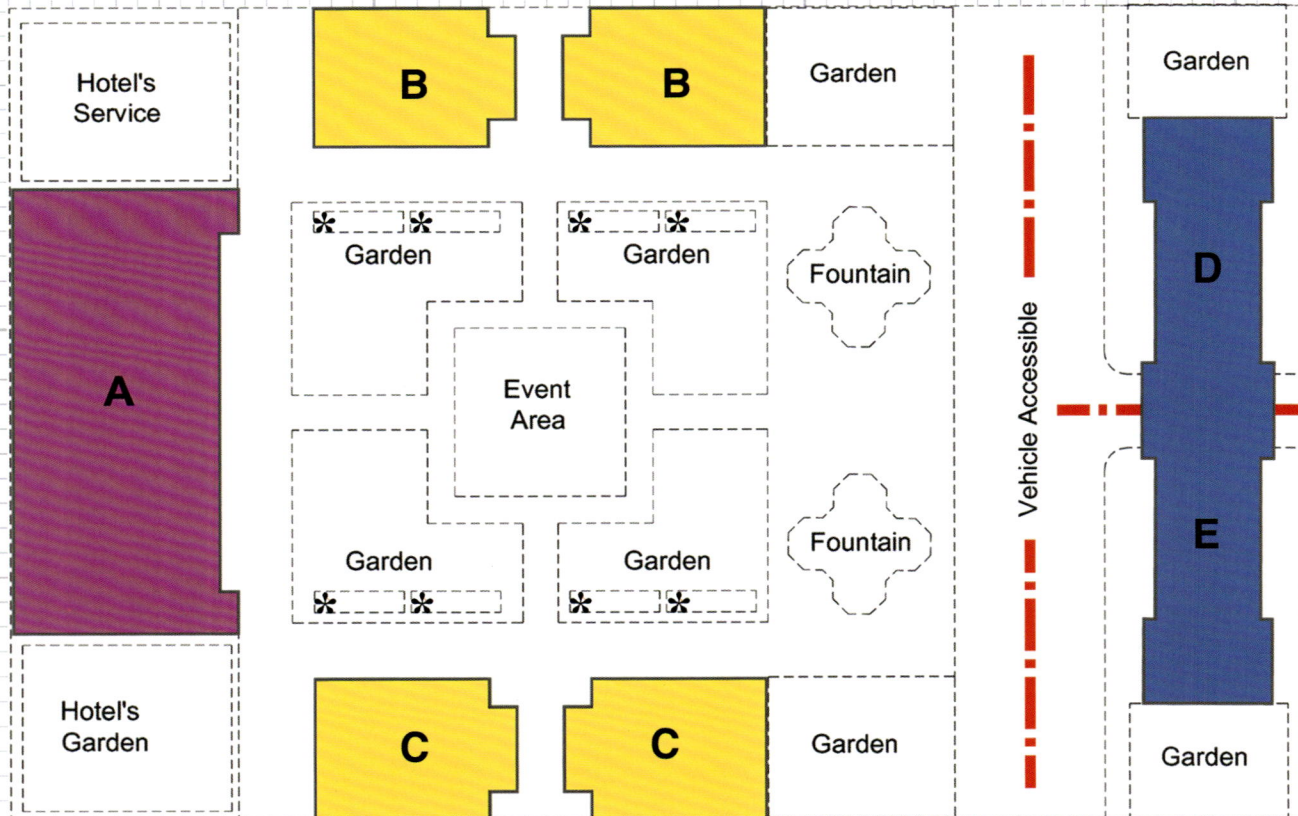

Hotel's Service	B B Garden
A	Garden Garden Fountain
	Event Area
	Garden Garden Fountain
Hotel's Garden	C C Garden

Garden

D

Vehicle Accessible

E

Garden

*Outdoor Covered Seating

ARCETRI PIAZZA PROTOTYPE #2 - GARDEN & EVENT PIAZZA
Planimetric Development Third Floor - Rooftop Garden

BUILDING A:

Area: 17,000 sq
Volume: 7.225 mc

Use:
Hotel Rooms, Swimming Pool
Roof Garden

BUILDINGS B-C:

Area: 3,700 sq. ft.
Volume: 1.580 mc

Use:
Building B - Apartments
Building C - Apartments

BUILDINGS D-E:

Area: 4,700 sq. ft.
Volume: 2.000 mc
Use:
Building D - Offices/Fitness
Building E - Offices/Apartments

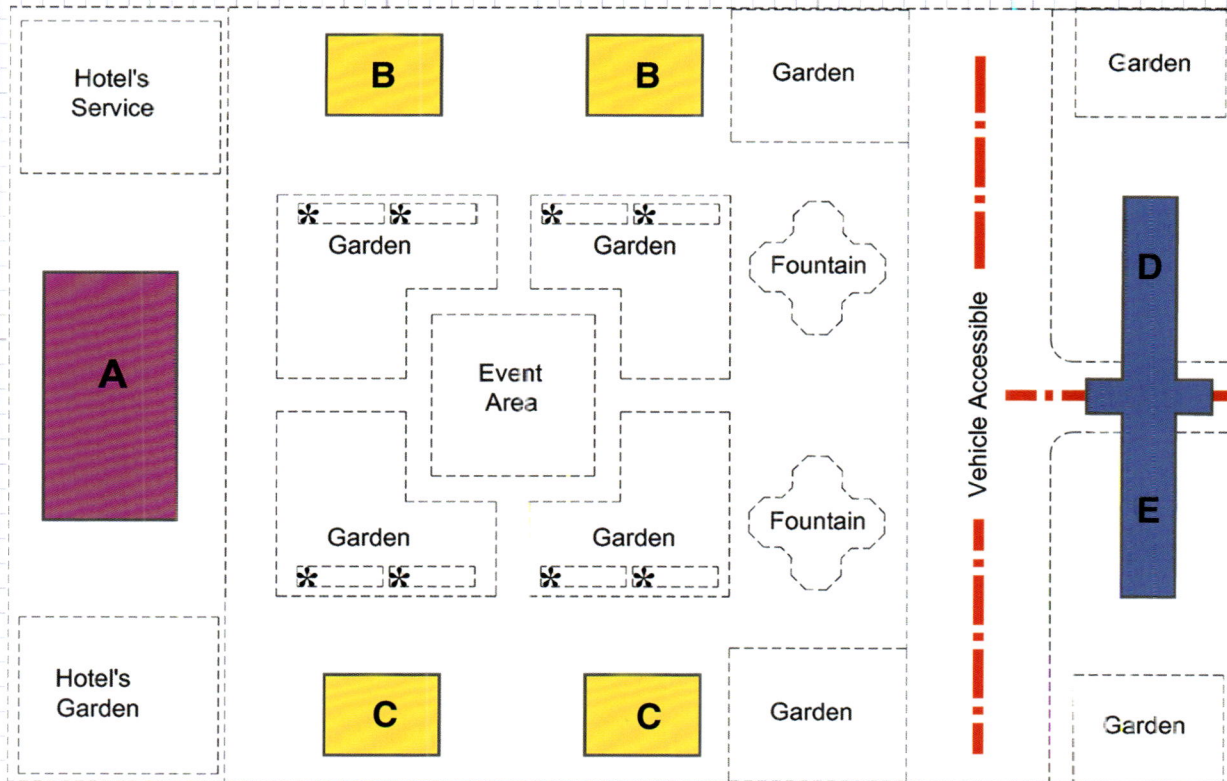

Hotel's Service

B

B

Garden

Garden

Garden

Garden

Fountain

D

A

Event Area

Fountain

E

Vehicle Accessible

Hotel's Garden

C

C

Garden

Garden

*Outdoor Covered Seating

ARCETRI PIAZZA PROTOTYPE #2 - GARDEN & EVENT PIAZZA
General Plan of the Area

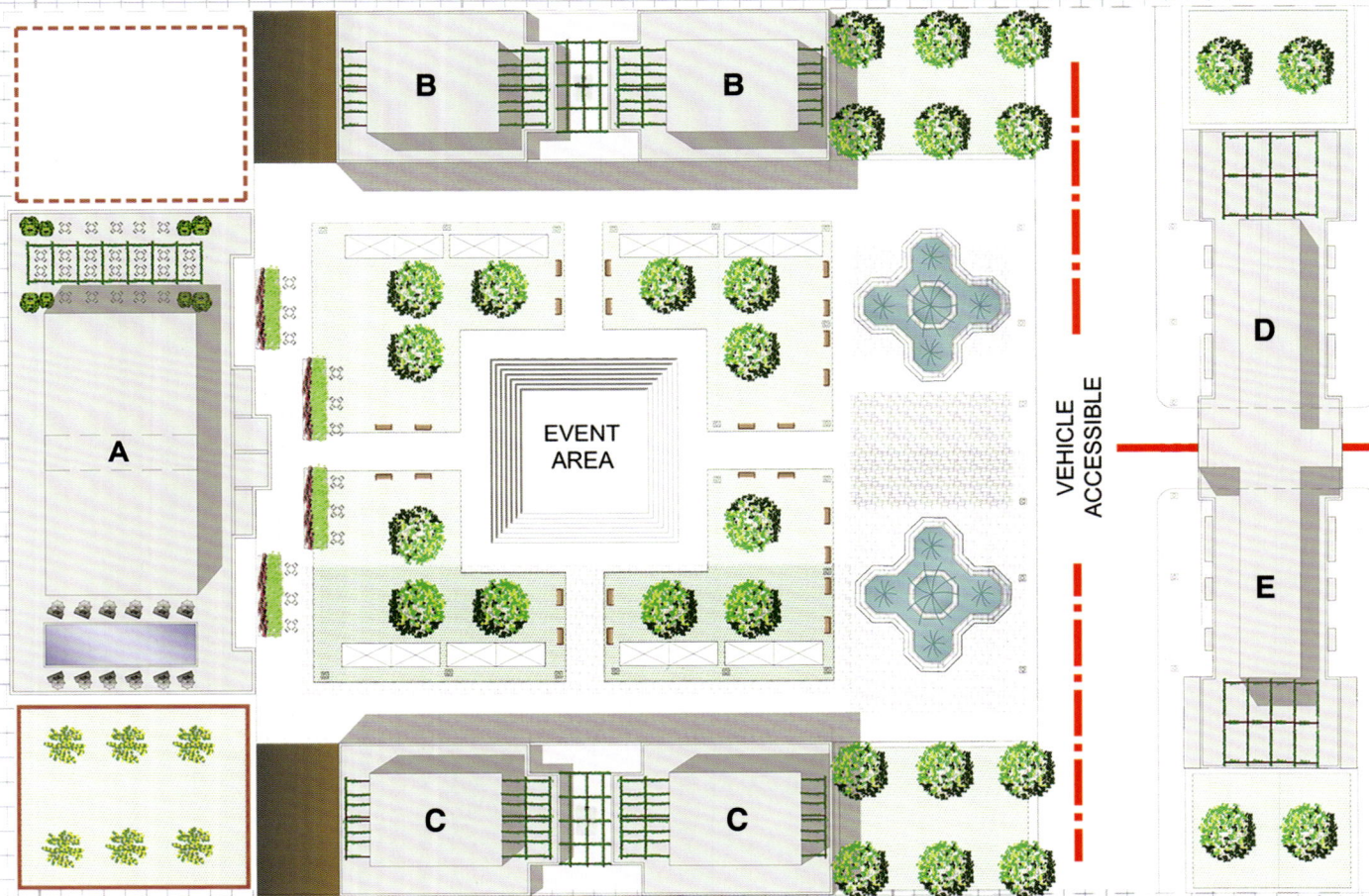

B

B

A

EVENT
AREA

VEHICLE
ACCESSIBLE

D

E

C

C

ARCETRI PIAZZA SAMPLE PROTOTYPE
Building A

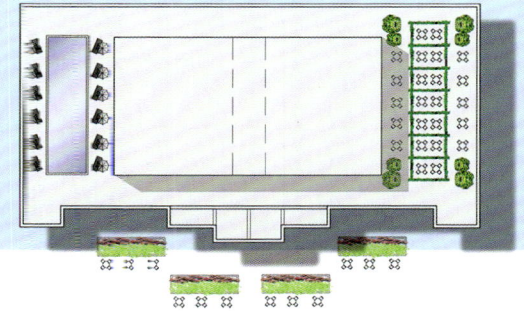

The Arcetri Piazza provides a unique lifestyle solution featuring Everyday Shopping & Living including Wellness/Fitness Resources.

There are a number of possible key anchors: Destination Restaurant, Hotel and Resort, Supermarket, Movie Theaters, Digital Nomad Work/Living Space, Corporate Village, Wellness/Fitness Center and/or an Integrative/Alternative Medical Center.

In the current real estate culture, the deeper value of life has been ignored.

The Arcetri Piazza represents a new asset class with a new mission: to provide everything people need to be happy, healthy and evolve. By addressing fundamental human connections and the multi-dimensional nature of life, the Arcetri Piazza becomes the central structural element of everyday living.

This is the idea of the Arcetri Piazza - Real Estate that provides a special atmosphere to bridge the gap between commercial viability and the highest levels of convenience, beauty and wellness.

131

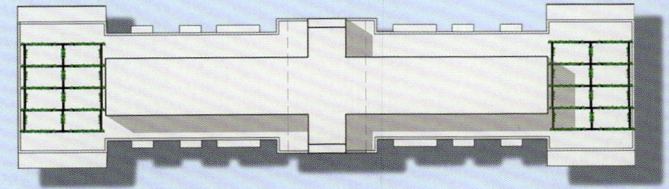

ARCETRI PIAZZA SAMPLE PROTOTYPES
Buildings B - C

The ARCETRI PIAZZA Buildings B and C remind us of a time when the power of emotional connection was based on shared experience.

The main building in Italian piazzas often features a classic clock tower as the point of reference and popular meeting place.

On the first floor of Buildings B & C there can be a variety of restaurants, including Farm-To-Marke Conventional, and Vegetarian/Vegan establishments.

This healthy food perfectly matches the Idea of the ARCETRI PIAZZA, as stated in the philosophy of the ancients: "Mens sana in corpore sano" (A healthy mind in a healthy body).

On the second and third floor there are apartments with spacious garden balconies.

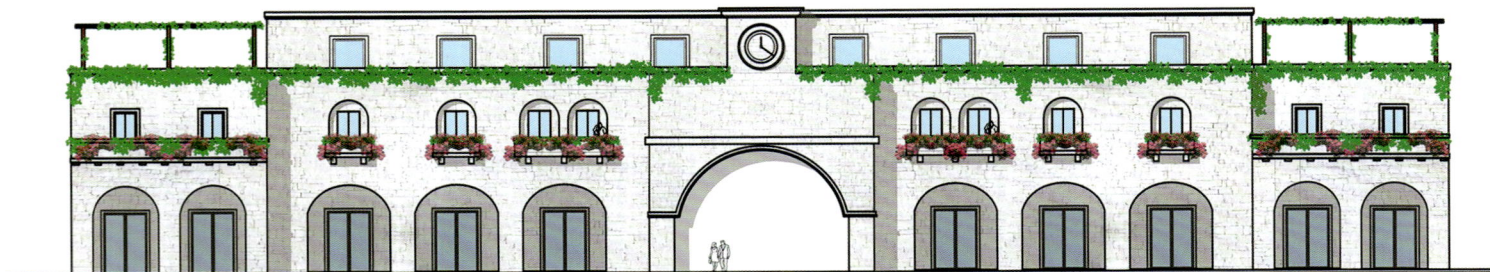

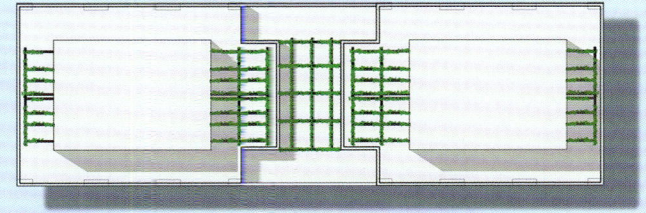

The ARCETRI PIAZZA Buildings D and E contain shops, apartments and offices, uniting the graceful tradition of a typical small Italian town with the amenities and services of a modern urban environment.

On the first floor there can be retail spaces anchored by a Supermarket, and including everyday essentials such as Post Office, Bank, Bakery, Dry Cleaner, Pharmacy, Bookstore/Cafe, and Medical/Dental.

The second floor can be divided between apartments and offices. Surrounded by greenery. The third floor offers ideal indoor-outdoor spaces for offices and apartments.

The Romeo & Juliet-style balconies located on the main facade evoke the timeless sensibility and human scale of the ARCETRI PIAZZA.

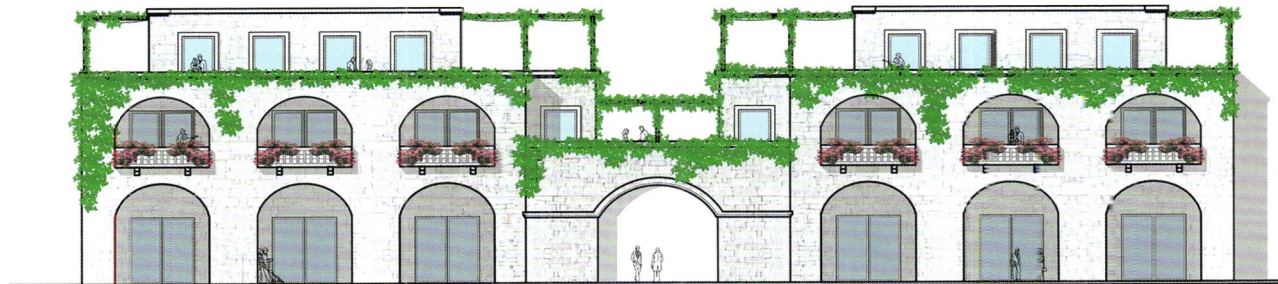

THE ARCETRI STORY

Arcetri is a small, semi-rural area located on the outskirts of Florence, Italy. It is the location of the Arcetri Observatory - a fully functioning astronomical research facility located near the Villa il Gioiello - Galileo's residence from 1631 until his death in 1642.

This was also an area frequented by many significant geniuses from the Florentine Renaissance: Leonardo da Vinci, Michaelangelo, Machiavelli, etc. Arcetri was one of the areas known for a number of the revolutionary developments of the Renaissance.

ARCETRI ITALIAN LIFESTYLE PIAZZA™

THE ARCETRI STORY

Arcetri, situated within the city limits of Florence, features the Villa del Poggio Imperiale, once the property of the Grand Dukes of Tuscany (Medici) and also the site of a memorable performance by Mozart in 1770. There are many beautiful villas and churches scattered across the Arcetri area, the most notable of the churches being the Church of San Leonardo.

135

Ten Questions Answered

10 QUESTIONS ANSWERED

Question 1. Why is our current transactional society transforming into an experiential/evolutionary society?

ANSWER: For the last 40 years, people's social and recreational experience outside the home has centered around dining, shopping, sports events and concerts.

The rising generation of Millennials have introduced a whole palette of interests, which puts a priority on experience and emotional connection ahead of purchases and other transactionally-based behaviors. The result is a demand for experiential environments which put a premium on social interaction. This demands a new type of built environment. The first phase of that transformation is the creation of specially designed central piazzas that anchor each community and create a balance between family life and community life.

The Arcetri Italian Piazza provides that solution – a solution which can be replicated across the U.S.A. and elsewhere.

Question 2. How does the Arcetri Piazza attract and enhance economic, physical, emotional and spiritual energy in a community?

ANSWER: The design and layout of an Arcetri Piazza influences the emotional and physical state of people. The entire experience of the Arcetri Piazza is designed to provide everything in one walkable place to accommodate a diverse range of tenants, clients and customers.

The proportions and layout of the Arcetri Piazza create an emotional field effect that stimulates an energizing sense of well-being and belonging. The welcoming outdoor spaces encourage people to slow down, mix and enjoy. The beauty and symmetry create an experience of harmony. This synergy of form and function naturally attracts people. The walking, human-scaled environment will generate intense foot-traffic. The proximity of a diverse array of goods and services creates an economic engine that can be stand-alone or part of a larger development.

Question 3. How is the Arcetri Piazza setting a new direction for the future success of commercial property?

ANSWER: The modern real estate investment community is restrained by two things: 1.) short-term thinking, and 2.) a limited subset of asset classes. Humanity is part of the past, the present, and the future, yet we continue to pretend that the future never comes. In fact, it is bearing down on us every minute and the increased velocity of change finds us unprepared.

When real estate became the color of money, truly creative thinking was lost and a transactional, cookie-cutter mentality took over. The incremental fixes used by commercial real estate today are inadequate to address the true nature of the fundamental shifts taking place in world culture. This paradigm change is similar to the shift that is now occurring as we transition from petroleum-based energy systems to renewable energy.

We need a completely different approach: we need to stop building for the short-term. We need to design buildings that last for generations.

ARCETRI ITALIAN LIFESTYLE PIAZZA™

Question 4. What is the effect of the Arcetri Piazza on human beings, society and the natural world?

ANSWER: For some time now, mankind has been acting as if we are separate from the vast, intricate, natural ecosystem that makes up our entire world on this beautiful jewel of a planet. This illusion of separateness has led to the creation of potentially disasterous imbalances within the natural environment, a world we totally depend on for our sustenance and survival. Currently, most of our public spaces and buildings are based on this separation-based, extraction economy.

The Arcetri Piazza concept provides a healing, corrective structure that is designed according to the deeper laws of nature, which humans have always been a part of. The present transactional mindset is inadequate to meet the challenges of our time. We can't return to the past, but we can create new ways of living and doing business that re-establish our interconnection with the natural world and the unseen, the emotional the transcendental.

Using ancient design techniques that enhance positivity, creativity and happiness, the Arcetri Piazza exerts a profound influence by creating a field effect that addresses all the needs and aspirations of human beings.

The Arcetri Piazza provides the perfect antidote to our present dilemma by establishing public spaces that are based on the deepest, most profound laws of nature, and because of that, support and encourage healthy, harmonious and creative lifestyles.

141

Question 5. How does the Arcetri Piazza avoid obsolescence?

ANSWER: The Piazza della Repubblica in Florence, Italy remains busy and fully occupied after centuries of continuous use. Current tenants include La Rinascente department store, the Apple Store and the Hard Rock Café, alongside historical cafes like Café Gilli (1733) and Café Concerto Paszkowski (1846).

When a commercial space is built in such a way that it spontaneously becomes part of people's everyday life, it will endure. When such a space gives people the joy of gathering and being together, it will generate an easy, frictionless experience every day, and it will generate profitable results for the developer and tenants. This revolutionary development concept will never go out of date because the fundamental human need for community and the enjoyment of being together is simply part of human nature.

Question 6. How do we re-establish the balance between private and public spaces ?

ANSWER: Everyone seeks community, friendship, and social interaction. As the present pandemic plays out across the world, people are rediscovering the joys and emotions of being at home with family. As the pandemic reshapes our daily routine, the way we work, shop and live will continue to evolve.

In the Italian tradition, the Arcetri Piazza has an abundance of outdoor space for meetings, dining, concerts and markets. As a central meeting place for the local community it has its own special, shared atmosphere.

143

Question 7. How does the Arcetri Piazza create connection?

ANSWER: The Arcetri Piazza is really the story of Memory. It is an ancient-yet-revolutionary template for a civic structure that expands the boundaries of individual life. The Arcetri Piazza re-awakens our connection to family, friends and the wider community. The piazza creates an energetic field that encourages the sharing of ideas and emotions, the building of friendships, the strengthening of shared destiny.

Question 8. How does the Arcetri Piazza make you feel?

ANSWER: The Arcetri Piazza is designed to invite you in. You enter the Arcetri Piazza as a welcomed guest.

When you walk into an Arcetri Piazza you are transported to a familiar place. The Arcetri Piazza has abundant light and outdoor spaces that allow for individual expression and enjoyment. It is a shared reference-point that creates emotional and spiritual equity.

145

Question 9. How does the Arcetri Piazza diminish loneliness and reconnect people?

ANSWER: The most captivating and restorative force on earth is love. It is medicine for the soul. Love and all its aspects: friendship, family connection, and romance continuously reconnects us with things that matter and help keep us healthy and happy. But, for love and friendship to flourish a context, a structure, is required. We live for the sense of participating in something bigger than ourselves. Living life this way is the greatest unifier. It inspires all the great journeys of life that lead to outer accomplishment and inner joy. It is the source of light that illuminates society. The effect of the structure of the Arcetri Piazza is to support, sustain and enhance these qualities of love and connection between people.

ARCETRI ITALIAN LIFESTYLE PIAZZA™

Question 10. What is special and unique about the Arcetri Piazza?

ANSWER: Most people mistakenly think a plaza and a piazza are similar. However they are not. A plaza is a place you walk through on the way to somewhere else. A piazza is a place that slows people down so that we can pause and enjoy the moment. The mindset of the modern world is that we are always going somewhere. This revolutionary real-estate development concept addresses that fundamental affliction of modern life by combining ancient design principles with the needs of the modern world. At the intersection of Art and Architecture, this design emerges from the most refined aspects of the human heart. Its underlying goal is as much about the journey of life as it is about economic success. The Arcetri Piazza fulfills the real and urgent need of our time by establishing a special, multi-purpose zone that provides the natural alignment of economic, societal and spiritual goals.

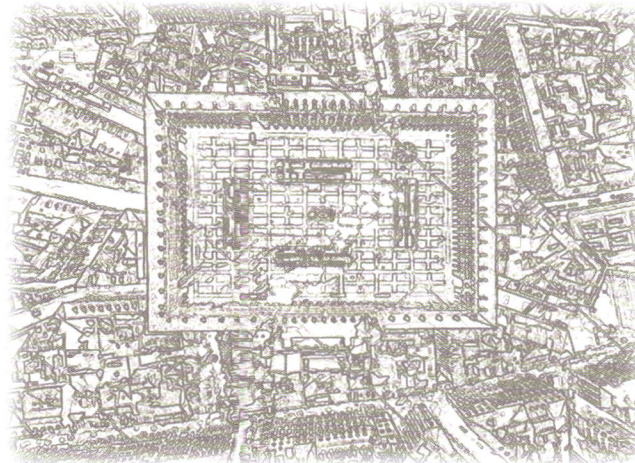

Most people commonly mistake a plaza for a piazza. A plaza is a place you walk through on the way to somewhere else. A piazza is a place that slows people down so that they may pause and enjoy life again.

"KNOW THYSELF"

Around the corner, just over the horizon, is a new world.

Centuries ago, humanity learned of new continents, new oceans, new places, but today's real estate mission is to help establish a culture based on the ancient saying, "Know Thyself."

ARCETRI ITALIAN LIFESTYLE PIAZZA™
BUILDING OUR FUTURE - THE JOURNEY AHEAD

Today we are in the midst of a global awakening.

We have reached the point where there is a massive wave of real estate obsolescence. The age-old human instinct to walk, to gather and share life has begun to take precedence over purely economic considerations.

The truest version of that ancient, human-centric lifestyle still lives on in Italy. After thousands of years, the desire to meet and gather at the piazza is still the focal point of life there. It continues to offer an entry point into every aspect of life from meeting your spouse, to acquiring an extended piazza family, to helping adolescents navigate the challenge of learning how to become part of a world outside their own immediate family.

Not long ago loneliness was an unknown malady in most cultures around the world, and the energy of human interaction gave most people a high level of emotional intelligence and elevated feelings. Italian words and concepts like: "simpatico" (congenial, nice) and "Fare a bella figure", (make a good impression) "va bene!" (everything's okay), or "la dolce far niente" (the sweetness of doing nothing) embody the idea of "la dolce vita" (the sweet life or the good life).

By default, Facebook, Twitter and Zoom have become the tech version of the world's piazza, and Amazon, the online shopping equivalent of the local marketplace.

BUILDING OUR FUTURE - THE JOURNEY AHEAD

The tech giants have esentially provided the world with an international meeting place and, in the process, habituated us to the convenience and genius behind their technology. In reality though, one of the unintended side-effects of these technological conveniences has been to make people feel more isolated.

We have friends halfway around the world, but when we walk down our own neighborhood street, we encounter mostly strangers. We struggle with a sea of unintended consequences springing up everywhere despite the technocrats' promise that every problem has an engineered solution.

Climate change, pandemics, loneliness, family breakdown, income inequality, new lifestyle diseases, and depression can be defeated only by returning to a deeper understanding what makes us tick. This includes a healthy diet, exercise, and true friendships - qualities that allow these qualities to flourish.

Each person ought to have the opportunity to enjoy their day in the process of making significant contributions to their own well-being and to society at-large.

A network of Arcetri Piazzas will be built around the U.S.A. and elsewhere. As we use these energetic common spaces over time, we will begin to live the memory of what it felt like to be together. This will stimulate the emotions and sense of common destiny and caring that was always the hallmark of every great human endeavor. This will support our ability to see each other as a gift,

BUILDING OUR FUTURE - THE JOURNEY AHEAD

as a potential friend - a source of energy and well-being. Like all natural healings, this transition will take time. The Arcetri Piazza lifestyle is a shortcut to a more balanced, happier world.

Around the world there is a awakening in every field of life. This is the most amazing time to be alive and to witness (and participate in) the world's coming together as we work to solve the challenging problems of our time. This is accomplished by creating a society that honors both values of life: the outer material world and the inner world of mind, emotions and consciousne

ABOUT THE AUTHOR

Barry B. Scherr is a commercial real estate developer, investor, author, and speaker on human potential and the built environment. He is the creator of a new asset class: the Arcetri Italian Lifestyle Piazza. Mr. Scherr is the Co-Founder of the Sundar Corporation, a national commercial real estate sale-leaseback company. He was an early pioneer in sale–leasebacks for the nationwide rollout of big box retail.

As president of Sundar Corporation, he developed a fast-track, multi-property approach to sale-leaseback transactions that established many of the standard practices used today. For the last 25 years, he has extensively studied how changing lifestyles and culture are transforming the way we live and what we build. In early 2020 Mr. Scherr created a transformational new asset class: the Arcetri Italian Lifestyle Piazza, which he is now rolling-out around the U.S.A. and other countries. He is assembling an international team of experts to make this happen. This new asset class features a completely re-imagined piazza for every locale that will revolutionize the way people meet, live, shop and play.

Everything about the Arcetri Italian Lifestyle Piazza concept is designed to provide a home for the new wellness-oriented, conscious lifestyle that is a bridge between the intimacy of the historical, antique city-centers of Italy, modern technological conveniences, and the joy of being together. Mr. Scherr splits his time between the United States and Italy. He has been a practitioner and teacher of Transcendental Meditation™ for the past 45 years. Barry is also a hobby producer of olive oil and organic vegetables.

For more information contact us at: barry@arcetripiazza.com

153

Special thanks to all the friends who generously offered their encouragment, inspiration and insight over the course of writing this book.

Michael W. Barnard

Barbara Bartolozzi
Gianluca Castaldo
John Clark
Larry Delrose
Eddie and Ina Drieband
Lisa Gerard
Tom Gould
Tom Mullins
Paolo Porcelli
Kristi Lynn Ricci
Mary Waldon
Anonymous Via Condotti Shop Clerk

Book Design and Editing
Michael W. Barnard/BoltPIX Studios
Santa Fe, New Mexico

Principal Photography
Michael W. Barnard

Additional Photography
Kristi Lynn Ricci

Architectural Renderings
Matteo Baroni, Chiara Benedetti
Matteo Baroni Architetto, Florence, Italy
Mara Modesti, Patricia Vaquero
Graff3D, Cordoba, Argentina

Stock Images
iStockPhoto.com
The Internet Archive www.archive.org
storyblocks.com
dreamstime.com